Cristiana Moldi-Ravenna • Tudy Sammartini

Secret Gardens in Venice

Photographs by
Gianni Berengo Gardin

translated by
Joseph A. Precker
Tudy Sammartini

arsenale editrice

Cristiana Moldi-Ravenna • Tudy Sammartini
SECRET GARDENS IN VENICE
Gianni Berengo Gardin

translated by
Joseph A. Precker
Tudy Sammartini

originally published as
Giardini Segreti a Venezia
by Cristiana Moldi-Ravenna and Tudy Sammartini
photographs by Gianni Berengo Gardin
© Copyright 1988 – 1992

printed in Italy by
EBS Verona

first edition
October 1996

second edition
April 1997

third edition
May 2001

fourth edition
December 2005

Arsenale Editrice
A division of EBS
Via Monte Comun, 40
I-37057 San Giovanni Lupatoto (VR)
Sito Internet: www.arsenale.it
E-mail: arsenale@arsenale.it

ISBN 88-7743-169-5

Table of Contents

9   PREFACE
    by *Vittorio Fagone*

13 SENTIMENT AS PROTAGONIST
    15 Memory
    30 The Hiding Place
    38 Confidences

53 RITES OF CELEBRATION
    55 Seals
    56 Self-Representation
    70 Ornaments

83 THE METAMORPHOSIS OF THE CITY
    85 Simples
    96 Repositories
    102 Meditation

111 THE HIDDEN CALL OF THE GARDEN
    113 Imaginary
    124 Spectacular
    136 Arcane

143 THE PRESENCE OF THE ABSENT
    145 Initiation

157 BIBLIOGRAPHY

163 INDEX OF NAMES AND PLACES

165 THE SITES

Of all the reflected and liquefied things in Venice and the number of these is countless, I think the lapping water loves them most. They are numerous on the Canalazzo, but wherever they occur they give a brush to the picture and in particular, it is easy to guess, give a sweetness to the house. Then the elements are complete – the trio of air and water and of things that grow. Venice without them would be too much a matter of the tides and the stones...

Henry James, *Italian Hours,* p. 43

The art historian, R.B., from Lausanne, has demonstrated that museums can be places full of life, where communication can thrive, and he is now concerned about the future of art in an age of technology. Over the last fifteen years I have run into him regularly, in places like Lucerne, the Ticino, Argentina, Canada, Paris, New York, and of course, Venice. Wherever we meet, we come up against the question of whether art can survive in this Age of Technology. Is it possible for the synthetic images of the electronic and computer age to be humanised by the culture of the West?

Both R.B. and I circle the globe in hope rather than pessimism. We are patient, knowing that research occasionally leads to good results. We search for some sign of creativity connecting the past and the future.

R.B. is a great conversationalist, as clear as Descartes, and as critical as Voltaire. With his charm and lack of pedantry, he has the qualities of an eighteenth-century *savant*, even though he is actively involved with the most recent problems in art, aesthetics, and social concerns.

I preserve a clear memory of one of our chance meetings in Venice, in a small out-of-the-way hotel between the church of Madonna dell'Orto and the hospital. The hotel had a long hall with a high curved ceiling that led out to a garden with a wide-open space stretching out to well-pruned trees behind which lay a boundary of strange artificial hillocks. With only the distant lights from the entrance illuminating us, our voices in the garden were clearer than our faces. In this special atmosphere, the discussion was animated, incisive, and marked by the clarity of R.B.'s comments, cutting through the dark. In the thick shadows of this unusual Venetian garden, I had the very real feeling that we were participating in a ritual that had been carried out before, as in some old and now obscure game. The following day we explored the garden, which was built around two artifices: the dwarf hills and pathways, and a Palladian construction on the lagoon, abandoned and desolate.

The memory lives on, but the Madonna dell'Orto Hotel is closed now. So typical of Venice. The past can live on indefinitely, or, in an instant, disappear completely...

This uniquely memorable garden is now unwalkable, overgrown, its contours lost in neglect, but my mind retains its dense shadows, and the lively voices of that evening, long ago.

From this fascinating and extraordinary book I learned that the Patarol, that very same garden, was once one of the great and secret gardens of Venice. At one time it contained a hundred and eighty kinds of roses, trees, plants and rare and precious flowers. Among those unusual artificial hillocks many other secret games had been played, against a background of esoteric and intellectual conversation.

The Venetian garden, like many another bordered and contained space, is a site for theater, grace, secrecy, and erudite or worldly conversation, as well as a place where the natural world metamorphoses into a controlled environment.

Philosophers have long sought to understand the fascination of gardens, enclosed or screened by architecture. One plausible explanation they offer is that the secret garden upsets the usual relationship between nature and architecture. Architecture, when surrounded by nature, makes its own statement, showing off its own non-organic form, its own artificial design. Nature, when intersected by architecture, reverses the situation and adds the element of surprise, the fascination of the unexpected, constructing a non-symmetrical viewpoint, no matter how ordered the garden or the house might be. This point of view is applicable whenever architecture and growing things meet. However, Venice has other elements that must be recognized: the miraculous meeting of stone and water, as John Ruskin has presented in his classic, *The Stones of Venice*. Water defends Venice; water, in its obedience to lunar patterns, gives a special rhythm to the city (as anyone who experiences *acqua alta* knows); water, in its perpetual motion, sets Venice in the flow of centuries... The organic nature of the canals, the movement of the boats, the human interaction with water, stone, history are all convergences that Ruskin dwelt on lovingly.

For Henry James, the Venetian garden was something else again; he saw it as the natural complement to the Venetian landscape, growing out of the intricate ambiguity of the lagoon, with its merging of sea and land.

Gianni Berengo Gardin, as is well known, is a photographer who has shown a remarkable ability to grasp the image of Italian cities in all their diversity, their sudden revelations and marvels. His explorations in Venice, without false rhetoric or emphasis, have captured the incredible orderly disorder of architecture, ornamentation, vistas, stones, water, unexpected details – and gardens. In these photographs Venice appears both time-worn and timeless. His skies curve like cupolas; architecture intrudes on greenery, and gardens enhance architecture.

The authors of this intriguing book have followed a strategy whereby the photography is integrated with two complementary modes and styles of research. Cristiana Moldi-Ravenna has devoted years of research to the idea of the city as a rational evolution. As a result, she has been able to discern relations between distant European cities both within and beyond certain styles (for example, the Baroque) since she discovers significant connections, rather than mere similarities.

Tudy Sammartini, from another vantage point, brings an intimate, affectionate, and involved awareness of the very special qualities of Venice, both in terms of its past, about which she is extremely knowledgeable, and its present. Awareness of the contemporary world of architecture combined with clear convictions serve to balance her approach to Venice and to gardens. Her knowledge and intuition are often backed up by rare and priceless documents known only to her. Living gardens, rare gardens, gardens long-abandoned, profaned, or destroyed – all appear to her as symbols of Venice's other face, changing with the seasons, with Time, doubly isolated from view by barriers of stone and trenches of canal water, yet serving not as background, but as backstage to the shifting urban scenery of Venice.

Like the various forms of the stones of Venice, the gardens have many shapes, many varieties. This book, in a sense, provides a kind of unique, reasoned history of Venice, revealing the connections with, and the differences from the great gardens of the Veneto hinterland.

However, it is not simply a history of Venetian gardens (which started out as orchards and vegetable gardens, a product of necessity, rather than aesthetics) but instead provides a kind of topographic and literary guide to Venice – setting the city along an unusual and fertile 'earth-line'. The result is a truly three-dimensional view of the lagoon city. The authors and the photographer transform the gardens we often sense, 'on the other side of the wall', into a kind of reality, which nonetheless still maintains a sense of mystery. The gardens are truly gardens of meditation, places for secret contemplation, secret meetings, secret personal thoughts and feelings,

emblematic of the special harmony and quality of Venice.

To add my own personal note, I myself have many memories of summers spent in the thick shade of Sant'Elena in my various roles at the Biennale. The unknown 'ordinary' gardens of the Giudecca also come to mind, green and vibrant. This is Venice – filled with the unexpected. It would be marvellous to count the trees, bridges, canals, the branches overhanging silent walls that I have passed in Venice, striding along at night with the painter E.V., the boats already 'at rest', walking along Calli known only to true Venetians...

To conclude with a more recent memory, I confess to having observed this elegant book take gradual shape, with Malcolm Lowry's words from *Under the Volcano* ringing in my ears, as an admonition, a counterpoint, an explanation: '¿Le gusta este jardin que es suyo? ¡Evite que sus hijos lo destruyan!'

Vittorio Fagone

Sentiment as Protagonist

MEMORY. 'Climbing up, therefore, step by step to Him that made me, I will pass beyond this faculty of my nature and come to the fields and wide pavillions of Memory... Great is the power of Memory, Lord; an astonishment, a deep and boundless manifold. Yet this also is mind and I am this. What am I, Lord? What is my kind? Even a life that changes and hath many modes and cannot in any wise be measured. The fields, the caves, the dens of Memory cannot be counted; their fulness cannot be counted nor the kinds of things counted that fill them... I force my way in amidst them, even as far as my power reaches, and nowhere find an end' (ST. AUGUSTINE in C.S. LEWIS, *The Allegory of Love*, p. 65).

Living in a city that is itself the accumulation of a millennium-and-a-half of incredible 'Memory' is forever fascinating, but also difficult, since public and private lives intertwine so inextricably, while each maintains its own special perspective. Life in Venice cannot be compared with that of any other city, and therefore it is not possible for those who have not lived in Venice, or at least visited it, to fathom its very special uniqueness. 'Streets' of water; streets that end nowhere; narrow passages that cannot be avoided, going from one place to another, no matter how crowded they may be... These are but a few of the infinite devices that serve to confuse, waylay, disorient the visitor. Venice is a city that protects its own privacy obsessively. Everywhere there are secrets within secrets.

The most secret place of all is the Venetian garden. There are far more gardens than one might guess, hidden away behind walls, behind palaces, beyond the canals. An aerial view of Venice always surprises the uninitiated, since so much green appears. Often, a modest facade (and an imposing *palazzo*) may hide a large and mysterious garden, with walkways, balustrades, statues, rare trees and plants. Such spaces lead us to ask:
'Where are we? Regard – here is a group of laurels as noble as those in the wood of Parrasio. Where are we? Here is a line of cypresses, companions to those of Vincigliata. Where are we? Here is a pine that emulates those where dwell the chattering cicada and the crows of the Agro. We walk slowly on a grassy slope without talking, frightened to awaken what seem to be large crouching birds of Paradise, but which are in reality *arbores vitae*, with the south-west wind ruffling their feathers, of the color of the aloe leaves of the lagoon' (G. D'ANNUNZIO, *La Leda senza cigno*, p. 149).

Many houses and gardens in Venice contain marble columns, statues, stones, fragments and

Ca' Zenobio. 'Probably all I have described will remain a dream, but you know that there are delightful dreams and that time spent within them is never wasted', Selvatico, Lettere alla Sig.ra M.B.B*., p. 37.*

15

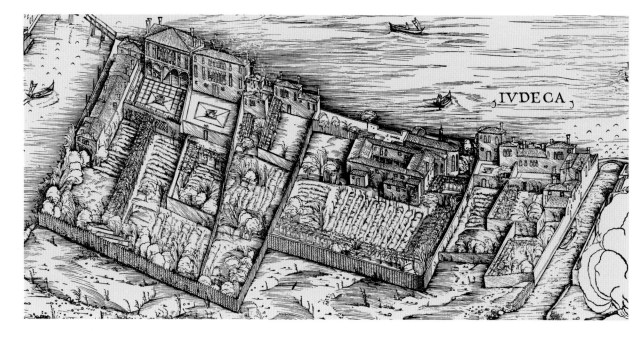

Detail of the plan of Venice drawn and engraved by Jacopo de' Barbari and published by Antonio Kolb in 1500.

16

exotic plants which recall the days when Venetian galleys sacked other cities around the Mediterranean, and brought back objects that seemed of value and of beauty. We still have many of these objects, adopted for quite different purposes and often difficult to identify or date, since they are sometimes copies of the original. What seems like a simple bench in a private garden may be an archaeological treasure. The stones, sometimes with inscriptions, come from far and wide.

It is curious how little Venetian gardens seem to be used. When one sees how barely they are furnished now, it is easy to imagine that they are abandoned. Today they are rarely a part of their owners' daily lives. In many cases what remains exudes a sense of decay or melancholy langour.

Many writers have pondered on the past life of these gardens. To find nature in the midst of such a densely built city is surprising, as if the Venetians were attempting to maintain the memory of the countryside, which lay near to them but was denied them by the barriers of water.

The only remaining garden that gives the impression of actually being in the open countryside is the Herion garden on the Giudecca. The enclosing trees separate it entirely from Venice, which seems very far away. Various ornamental plants add to the sensation of remoteness. The only confusing element is the Renaissance wellhead from the nearby former convent of Saints Cosmo and Damian.

One can get an idea of how Venetian spaces were used as gardens by looking at old maps of Venice, such as the one drawn and engraved by Jacopo de' Barbari and printed by the German,

Antonio Kolb, in 1500. This map provides a bird's-eye view accomplished by combining panoramic views from several belltowers, corrected by precise mathematical rules. The view presents Venice as seen from the sea with the Giudecca in the foreground, and reveals the whole city in infinite and iconographic detail in accordance with Renaissance taste. The open spaces are more clearly enclosed and compressed in the center of the city, and more ample at the edges.

On the Giudecca, facing the lagoon, the many large gardens are drawn meticulously, their water side protected by wooden stockades with the separation between terrain and lagoon not yet always clearly defined. The stockades hold back the tides, preventing valuable reclaimed land from slipping back into the ever-encroaching swamp. A continuous series of compact houses provide protection from the often-cruel north-eastern winds.

These houses open onto courtyards paved with tile and stone, with the indispensable well water, the symbol of life. A narrow pathway leads from the courtyard, onto a wide space before the lagoon. Fields, flowerbeds, vegetables, medicinal herbs, rose bushes, grapevines, jasmine, all laid out in clear geometric patterns, lead along a thick copse of trees backing up against the stockade that separates the cultivated areas from the water's edge. Today, the garden of Casa Frollo (sadly closed) still perfectly represents those drawn five hundred years ago by de' Barbari, with its paved courtyard and its well near the house, the garden beyond it, divided into large flowerbeds separated by a pathway, and finally, at the far end, the entrance to the vegetable-garden, while nearby a service door

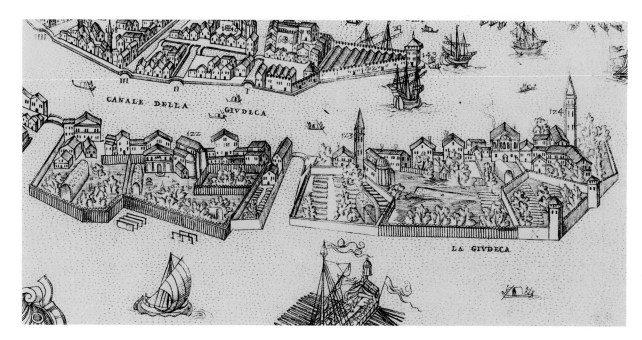

Detail of the map by Paolo Forlani engraved by Bolognino Zalterio, Venice 1566.

opens to the left, revealing a place for tools and other farm implements. The garden has little rose-trees laid out between the flowerbeds and the lawn.

Made fifty years later, Matteo Pagan's map accentuates the definition of the edges where the garden meets the water. The relations between buildings and open spaces have changed very little but now everything is completely enclosed. In addition to the pilings that aim to protect as much earth as possible, we find walls, towers, and peripheral buildings that protect the gardens on all sides. Now, the points at which the earth meets the water have been made more stable, as, for example, at San Giacomo, seen on Pagan's map. He even has a wooden structure, with laundry hanging out to dry. Another wooden structure acts as a landing-stage. This area has always been a place for vegetable and flower gardens.

'This garden belonged to English people who allowed visitors to promenade in it: the simplest garden in the world, without artificial perspectives; not designed by an architect; almost a vegetable garden. Beyond some small low houses, where Casanova would have been at ease, one proceeds along a narrow alley, between square beds of greens and flowers. A beautiful *mangifera* shone like a reliquary between the cabbages. Here and there, small, fresh-water basins for watering the plants glimmered faintly like Venetian glass mixed with ashes. Under hedges of Bengala roses, there were, discreetly hidden, the tombs of beloved dogs... Long shafts of horizontal light, which break through the skies of Venice, enliven the flower beds with shades of apricot and peach...' (J.L. Vaudoyer, *Les délices de l'Italie*, p. 128).

Today, we can find two gardens in this area. The Sacerdoti garden covers part of the area, where lady Layard founded the English hospital active until 1940 or so, described by Frederick Rolfe in *The Desire and Pursuit of the Whole.* The Sacerdoti house looks over the Fondamenta and Canal della Croce, where an iron bridge and a double gate mark the boundaries of the garden created by the Englishman Francis Eden (and often referred to as 'The Garden of Eden'). The walkway to the house opens onto a wide field with a pergola on the right that leads towards the pool and a semi-circular bench at the end, beyond the well-spaced trees. All this can be seen from the living room. Near the house, a sandbox and a children's red climbing frame give vitality to the space. From the roof terrace we can see the nearby vegetable garden of Ca' Leon and the thick, now-uncultivated underbrush of the 'garden of Eden'.

In traditional form, the Ca' Leon garden is divided into two distinct areas. What makes this garden unique is that it is the house itself that divides the space. Entering from the Fondamenta della Croce (from where it is impossible to see the vast expanse of green within) one reaches a *patio* that separates the main garden entrance from the entrance to the vegetable garden. The garden is beautifully groomed. An English lawn with tall cypresses takes up the main area in front of the house. On the left there are beds of flowers of many colors, separated by a pathway that leads to the raised *belvedere*, of brick and Istrian stone. The *belvedere* is covered by wisteria and Virginia creeper. Olive trees, laurel, *pistosforo*, interspersed with white stone benches, lead down to the water's edge along a little wall.

overleaf
In Lodovico Ughi's plan printed in 1729, great attention is paid to the exact design of the gardens.

ICONOGRAFICA RAPPRESENTATIONE
CONSACRATA AL REGGIO S

ALOYSIO
MOCENICO
VENETIARUM
DVCE

Veduta della Piazza di S. Marco dalla parte del mare

Veduta della Piazza di S. Marco verso S. Geminiano.

Procuratioe nuoue architettura di Vicenzo Scamozzi

Procuratioe vecchie architettura di Mastro Bono Bretz di S. Marco.

Veduta della Chiesa Ducale di S. Marco.

Veduta della Piazza di S. Marco verso la Chiesa Ducale.

Veduta della Piazzetta verso la Zecca.

Veduta delle Prigioni, architettura Sansovino

LEUANTE

PONENTE MAESTRO

FORENTE

SACCA DI S. CHIARA

ISOLA DI S. CHIARA

ISOLA DI S. MARTA

PUNTA DI S. BIAGIO

RIO TRE PONTI

CANAL GRANDE

CANAL DELLA GIUDE

SCALA DI PASSI CINQUE CENTO VENETI DA PIEDI CINQUE L UNO

SUCCINTE ANNOTATIONI DELLA QUI SOP.ᵗᵉ DELINEATA CITTA

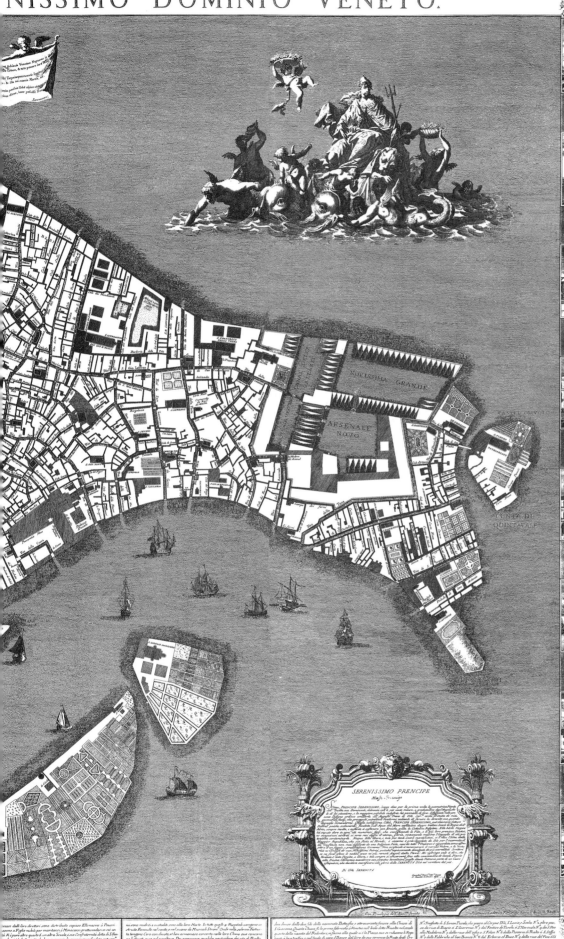

NOVISSIMA GRANDE

ARSENALE NOVO

CANAL OLIVOLO

PUNTA DI QUINTAVALE

SERENISSIMO PRENCIPE

*Detail of the area
of Sant'Elena from
the plan by Bernardo
and Gaetano
Combatti, 1847,
updated in 1855; it
provides clear evidence
of the efficiency
of the Hapsburg
administration.*

20

*The former 'garden of
Eden'.
'Its foliage is dark,
harsh and thick... from
the evergreen foliage
new leaves sprout at
regular intervals, alive
like lapping tongues'.
D'Annunzio,*
Notturno *p. 236.*

The pathway from the *belvedere* leads to the edge of the garden, where one can glimpse the nearby garden and orchards of the Franciscan friars behind the Palladian church of the Redentore. In correspondence to the opening to the vegetable garden beyond, there is a dovecote inhabited by white doves, as a reminder of the former 'house of roses and birds', as Damerini called it. The large vegetable garden has three vine-covered pergolas that run its entire length: there are also clusters of persimmon, pomegranate, and cherry trees. A statue of Adonis stands beyond the last pergola. Near the house, guarding the double entrances to the gardens, there are replicas of Greek statues. This garden has been much praised for its beauty. In a letter to its owner, Benedetto Cornaro, Pietro Aretino wrote: 'If the Giudecca were not admired for the beauty of its churches and its location, the verdant gardens surrounding your noble home by themselves would be proclaimed as a marvel' (P. ARETINO, *Lettere*, libro V, n. 122).

In the time of Cornaro, the two gardens were part of one property. Cornaro invited artists and writers, such as Maffeo Venier, Gian Luca Trissino, Pietro and Bernardo Bembo, Monsignor Giovanni della Casa, Titian, Ruzante, Donato Giannotti, Jacopo Nardi and Giovanni de' Medici, as well as Aretino.

By comparing various maps with that of Paolo Forlani, engraved in Venice in 1506 by Bolognino Zalterio, we note that high tide is emphasised. Water laps the city on every side, and even the Giudecca laundry poles are under water.

The same precision can be found in the depiction of several gardens. For example, there is the Bastianello garden of Palazzo Businello facing the Grand Canal. The garden is protected by a high wall that faces the Fondamenta. Inside, a porphyry walkway borders a lawn. A pine on the left and two fig trees are the only trees in the garden. All around, however, the walls of the houses are covered with woodbine, which shimmers delightfully in the tiniest breeze, while the terraces are decorated with the same plant, thereby breaking up the facade of the palace, which otherwise would be overwhelming.

*Herion garden.
'In 1866 the digging of
a well in an orchard
produced a column of
water, 40 meters high,
which damaged the
nearby houses, creating
hollows in the ground'.
Tassini,* Curiosità
veneziane..., *p. 8.*

*Abbazia della
Misericordia.
'A garden wall runs
along the other side,
over which I can see
pomegranate-trees in
fruit and pergolas of
wine...' Symonds,* New
Italian Sketches, *p. 172.*

The whole gives the sense of a tapestry, a wall covered by fabric.

We know, very clearly, that we have entered the so-called 'Age of Enlightenment' when we read the dedication on Lodovico Ughi's map of 1729: 'Here for the first time is the geometrical Map of the Illustrious Ruling City, delineated with the most careful measurements, and the precise degrees of all its angles, as its situation and the greatest possible industry permitted... this is the first fruit of my geometrical studies...'.

This is the first large-scale plan of Venice with the city represented in an ideal fashion, Ughi depicting the city systematically and analytically. The gardens are drawn with scientific care to detail. They are extremely numerous, and are concentrated on the Giudecca and along the edges of Cannaregio, like a continuous stretch of green, interrupted only by canals. In Ughi's map, greater attention is paid to the gardens than to the buildings, which are simply documented.

Today, at San Rocco, a sixteenth-century house opens out at the back like a country villa. The Salmistrari garden is carefully subdivided into flowerbeds by a central tiled walkway leading to the orchard further along, recalling the rigor with which Ughi drew his map.

Bernardo and Gaetano Combatti's map of 1847, updated in 1855, was the finest ever; with the perfection of its details it was a monument to the efficiency of the Hapsburg administration. Comparing it with Ughi's map we can see all the changes since 1797. The newly-built railway station and the long railway bridge connecting Venice with the mainland are clearly depicted. Waterways and walkways have been changed; monumental areas, convents, palazzi have been transformed. We can also see how areas that were considered peripheral before the link with the mainland have now been urbanized. Green areas are well documented and new kinds of gardens have been created as a result of confiscations, demolitions, and expropriations.

The garden of Palazzo Tiepolo is one of these new ones. Situated near the Fondamenta della Misericordia, today only the foundations and the corner-stones remain. Demolished between 1798 and 1800, the palace has disappeared, but there are still remnants of the garden, divided into two parts: one part is cultivated, the other wild, according to the tastes of their different owners. The world of the past is only faintly discernible here. Nonetheless memory is stirred:
'If I close my eyes, I still see the abandoned garden of Palazzo Gradenigo, a long and narrow garden, ending in a kind of portico with Palladian columns... Slender flowers offer perfume from flowerbeds. Pomegranates, as they ripen, grow fat. I walked there so slowly I feel as if I lived there years and years...' (H. DE RÉGNIER, *Esquisses vénitiennes*, p. 10).

The Basin of San Marco seen from the Giudecca. 'Merchandise runs through that town like water in a sluice. Venice, built on the sea, with water that runs through and around everything, except the homes and the streets. The citizens can return home by way of the land, or by way of water'. Da Canal, Les histoires de Venise, *part I, 2-4, p. 5.*

24

Today, in the Gradenigo garden, we find chairs, placed in a mysterious circle around an old weeping-willow tree. In many gardens in Venice objects of mystery turn up in the most unexpected places and ways, sometimes haphazardly, sometimes by design, recalling past occasions, never to be forgotten.

In the neighborhood of San Samuele, in the Alverà, Mocenigo and Bennati gardens, once interconnected, there are still vestiges of the taste for conserving treasured finds, even though they have been separated from their original settings: the confused-looking monkey carved in stone, the bearded head upon the ground in the Bennati garden, and the remains of a folly, are just some examples of this. Then there are the languid maidens with their carved draperies, the little dwarves, the inevitable Rape of the Sabine women, blocks of stone of various dimensions, obsessively piled in the tiniest of spaces behind the shrubbery on the left, in the grounds of the old Palazzo Mocenigo garden.

In the little Alverà garden, located halfway between the private courtyard with an external stairway and the main garden, the isolated Byzantine wellhead draws attention to itself.

In the Cosulich garden on the Dorsoduro, in contrast, it is the architecture that intrigues us, dominating and limiting the greenery. The garden itself appears as a long rectangle

beginning in front of the house with a paved area. A water basin reflects a series of statues, dressed in Oriental style and lined up along a wall that separates it from another garden, while on the right a long wooden pergola, held up by stone columns, is covered in vines. The central flowerbeds along the edges of the silhouetted basin draw the eye toward a large decorated door, a 'blind' door, leading nowhere.

Many gardens in Venice are like houses, protecting the occupants as do the walls of a house. Some of these gardens become, in effect, an additional room to the house, albeit a 'room' open to the sky and the sea. The small garden of Vittorio Fiorazzo on the Fondamenta Soranzo is a rectangle, filled with *trifolium repens* and surrounded on three sides by a paved pathway. Against a creeper-entwined background, we find a great Neptune – an eighteenth-century copy of an Alessandro Vittoria's statue. In its simple linearity, the entire garden is conceived as an extension of the main living room.

A little further on, small dividing walls of various heights animate the Calzavara garden, which is hidden, being wedged-in between two other gardens. This little garden is divided into three separate areas. In the center there is a Byzantine wellhead, shaded by thick laurels. Toward the back, on the right, an Art Nouveau mosaic with an urn hides the

Herion garden.
'Here it is like being
in the country, you can
enjoy all its pleasures.
No dust disturbs you,
no stomping horses,
no clattering wheels,
resound in your ears.
All you hear is the
murmur of the waves,
now and again
emphasised by the
plash of oars'.
Selvatico, Lettere alla
Sig.ra M.B.B.*, p. 17.*

25

storage place for firewood. On the right, a table and chairs form an extension of the house itself.

Comparing what we see today with the life of the past, one is so struck by the differences that one finds oneself asking the stock questions about Venice. Why is this city so intriguing? Writers, ancient and modern, have allowed themselves to be seduced by the charm and fascination that the water and the facades of the palaces have always exerted on the visitor.

The reflections of the buildings in the water, the various colors that bounce off the surface of the canals, the ever-changing light create a unique ensemble of nature and architecture, the organic and the man-made. In dealing with Venice, we often find it necessary to anchor ourselves in her past, even though her lost greatness and complex history evoke in us only profound melancholy. Venice is always the same, and yet forever new, since her seasons, her skies, her waters, her moods, her palaces, byways, bridges belong to herself and to herself alone, leaving the spectator, no matter how world-weary and *blasé* elsewhere, in awe and open to surprise. In a way, it is best for the visitor to remain tongue-tied, allowing Venice to speak for herself, to express herself through the coats-of-arms that still hang on the walls of restored or decaying palazzi, clamouring for

recognition. The natural elements that creep into the crevices of ancient stones testify to an irrepressible will to survive; the whole city seems to live on, supported only by the crutch of its own past.

The spontaneous flora is the living memory of Venice and even along the Calli we encounter rich undergrowth, with ferns and mountain plants that have followed the stones from the quarries of Istria, and which hide their seeds wherever possible, to germinate a new each year. Other plants have fled the botanical gardens to become ornamental houseplants. Others bring to mind the forests that have been destroyed by time, like the *Selva Fetontea* on the edge of the lagoon. Mediterranean species flourish in Venice too, such as the evergreen oak, the laurel, and the oleander, brought from afar.

'– Stop in front of Palazzo Vendramin-Calergi! – he ordered the gondolier. Passing along the walls of the orchard, he grabbed some frail flowering plants growing in the cracks of the bricks. The flowers were the color of congealed blood, violet, of extreme delicacy, and impalpable... He thought of the myrtle growing along the coast of the Aegean, as proud and harsh as bushes of bronze. He thought of the dark cypresses topping stony hills of Tuscany, and the tall laurels protecting the statues in the villas of Rome' (G. D'ANNUNZIO, *Il fuoco*, p. 206).

Zieseniss garden at San Sebastiano.
'Once, in Venice, there were many vineyards cultivated by gardeners, who did not belong to a guild but a special group of farmers cultivating the fields of Castello, Vignole, Giudecca and Cannaregio'.
Tassini, Curiosità veneziane..., *p. 717.*

26

Matteo Raverti, external stairway in Palazzo Contarini with the Iron Gate.

In addition to the expected relics you find when visiting the gardens of Venice, such as broken columns, statues, plaques, you can also find surprising things which become beautiful precisely because they are worn, useless, and no longer fulfil the function they were made for.

Wherever there is uncultivated greenery, as for example on the Giudecca, it is possible to find fragments of broken ancient pottery, relics of a former age, and even stage backdrops used at some long-distant event. Nature, like Time, levels all things, and unless guided by the hand of man, can become an Enemy.

It is the necessity to control and construct Nature that makes the Venetian garden an entity unto itself. For many of them we have only a written record of the original plans or diagrams, and therefore any comparison between past and present can only be fragmentary. Yet memory leaves some of its traces in stone, for those who search hard enough to find them...

Gardens in Venice were much more numerous in the past. When neglected, or no longer in use, gardens can disappear very quickly.

In former times, even in some regal gardens, as well in most gardens of Venice, some part of the garden was an *orto* (a kitchen garden) providing fresh fruit and vegetables for the houshold. Of course, in the present day, with fruit and vegetables from all over the world readily available, this need has almost disappeared. In former times, the garden, was protected from intruders with high walls, some of them crenellated at the top, resembling the castles of medieval Europe in a simple style for humble homes, a more elaborate one for the palazzi. Walking along the Calli, we can still see examples of crenellation, from the vast wall surrounding the Brandolin garden to the tiny Lazzarini garden. This latter, near San Barnaba, consists of two separate areas. The first, which you enter by the large door giving onto the Calle, is a square of lawn with a fountain in the center. Once you enter the portico, on the right, there is a large fig-tree, many ornamental plants and statues. The greenhouse on the left is in active use, with a crenellated wall that separates it from the adjacent garden. Care and cleanliness reign; the atmosphere is so fresh, it hardly seems European.

The crenellation on the garden wall blocks access and symbolizes protection and retreat from the world outside.

In many of the paintings of Antonello da Messina, Carpaccio, and Bellini, the cusps of the crenellation become elegant amphorae holding plants and flowers that suggest an extension of the garden rather than a separation from it. We can still find examples

*The Lion guarding
the Terra garden
at the Accademia.*

30

previous pages
*Calzavara garden
'a tiny basin... in its
round water it looked
like a liquid rose, a
yellow rose that had
opened too far'.
De Régnier,* Italie
Septentrionale, *p. 140.*

of this, in Calle Ca' Foscari, for example where stone amphorae and stone flowers ornament a dividing wall.

The Fullin garden is another unexpected discovery. It is of the kind that serves as an extension of the *salotto*, the room for entertainment and relaxation. Such spaces acquire an elegance found nowhere else. In the center of the Fullin garden, there is a wooden pergola covered with wisteria, supported by graceful columns of Istrian stone. Emerging from the house, and walking towards the back of the garden, it is possible to enjoy a classical perspective, underlined by the play of the light on the wooden trellis ready to host the climbing rose – now, like so much of Venice and its gardens, notable by its absence.

THE HIDING PLACE. This city, built in the water, with its repetitive structure of Campi, tortuous little streets and countless bridges, is a single nucleus in which life goes on in the same way, everywhere. Public life and private life interact ambiguously.

When one emerges from a palace, or a simple home, the impression is that of entering an environment of familiar faces and daily rituals, where neighbors and strangers look at one curiously, interested to know who one is, what one is doing, where one is going. The inhabitants of Venice seek to defend their privacy by creating their own private spaces.

The curiosity of Venetians is endless, while on the one hand, desiring privacy and respecting the desires of others for living their own lives, on the other hand, Venetians tend to cast furtive glances at the comings and goings of their neighbors – and of strangers as well – wondering what complicity is afoot, how the next person is trying to establish a foothold that may damage the self-interest of the onlooker; what new affair has begun...

In a sense, long ago – and even today –, much of life in Venice resembles a Goldoni play...

The gardens are always designed around a structure of three clear-cut spaces: one part is a typical Italian formal garden, paved with a geometrical design, another is reserved for the enjoyment of nature, the third part, perhaps the most important, is the secret garden, with gazebos and quiet corners, perfect for meditation and secret meetings.

Most Venetian gardens are inaccessible. And even the few people who are allowed entry will seldom have access to the most secret part of the garden, which is reserved for fantasy and dreams, which must be kept from the prying eyes of strangers, gossips, and even from other family members. Venetians are eager to protect their private worlds, so that their memories and their dreams maintain

Orsoni garden,
vats to mix the colors
for the mosaic tiles.

31

their magic. Gardens are custodians of deep feelings, not only proud and vain thoughts, but also sentiments that are simple and eternal.

For a Venetian the most important path in the garden is the one that leads us to the secret hiding places. In every corner of the garden memories linger on: lost loves, departed relatives, men and women who played important roles in our lives, all of these are still present in every stone in our gardens. Ghosts of memory, fantasies only, but they will remain alive until the stones themselves crumble.

Such secrets are more difficult than ever to protect. In 1984 color aerial photographs were made of the whole city so that every roof, every open space, every street, canal, bridge and even every garden was recorded.

Only from above is it possible to reveal the secrets of the maze in heart form in the garden of Palazzo Brandolin, the charming double S of the plantings in the Tagliapietra garden, the exact geometrical form of the flower beds of the Grimani garden. While the aerial map of Venice makes everything look sharp, clear-cut and accurate, the old maps remain more interesting, because they represent personal interpretations of the artists who drew them.

In the Seminary of the Salute the visitor is greeted by shade: the sun is filtered by dense foliage and the earth is damp and covered with moss. The space is not particularly extensive, but looks wider because there is an artificial hillock in the center. The garden does not follow the eighteenth-century plan of Ughi but that of Combatti. Access to the garden is by way of an external stairway behind the main building of the Seminary. To the left a sinuous pathway defines the boundaries of the garden. A herringbone pattern of bricks captures our attention with their unusual texture. Here and there lie pieces of old marble, some with inscriptions worn away by time and the elements. All of these are remnants of convents, churches and monasteries, destroyed at the beginning of the 19th century. Halfway up the miniature hill there are a table and benches in a cercle, made of Istrian stone, around which the seminarians gather at specific times to meditate and to pray.

Not far away, there is a statue of the Madonna, for the contemplation of the woshipper...

Further on, there is a pergola covered with vines. Beyond that there is a sunny open space, where the Seminarians play football. Nevertheless, the overall feeling that the garden instils is one of peace and repose.

This need for restful separation from the world was well depicted by D'Annunzio: 'In the Calle Gambara, near the Accademia there is the cloister where a woman, on the point of losing her beauty, gave a great party,

*Ca' Leon.
Venice was originally
an agricultural zone.
In Augustus's time,
the Lagoon was
probably divided by a
barrier of dunes into
two separate areas, with
land on one side and
water on the other.*

32

*Ca' Leon.
'There are certain
statues, fauns and
nymphs, which weather
stains and mosses have
made much decenter
than the sculptor
intended'. Howells,*
Venetian Life, *p. 87.*

and then retired, behind the doors of her home,
now hermetically sealed, forever... so that no
one would ever see again her vanishing beauty...
The shutters are closed. Everything is silence
and mystery. Only the birds, on the trees,
continue to sing' (G. D'ANNUNZIO, *Taccuini*,
p. 106).

The garden still exists behind the Palazzo
Basadonna Recanati, now the Liceo Artistico
near the Ponte delle Maravegie near the
Accademia. From the entrance hall we can see
the garden with its undulating mounds which
give the aspect of a romantic hilly terrain. At the
far end of the garden there is a door in a high
wall that leads to the Accademia.

On the Giudecca there is a very special
garden created on the site of an old orchard.
One enters through a courtyard with an ancient
wellhead covered with rambling roses. In this
rectangular space two pathways run along two
walls thickly covered with vines, and through
the thick verdant foliage one catches the
reflection of the blue water of the
swimming-pool. Beyond the swimming-pool,
protected by pines, cypresses, cedars, laurels,
and chestnut-trees there is a semicircular
structure, used as a dressing room, whose
mirrors multiply the blue of the pool and the
green of the arbor. In the center there is a
rose-covered *berceau*. The beautiful red roses
emphasize the whiteness of the marble of the
ancient statues of Venus and Adonis. The lawn

continues with a paved area on the other side of
which there is the guest pavilion. The privacy of
this well-conceived area is underlined by the
fact that from no point is it possible to see the
overall lay-out of the garden. The mystery is
enhanced by old statues, antique vases, and the
remains of old capitals from palaces and
temples destroyed long ago.

It is characteristic of Venetian gardens that
the most attractive part of the garden is
protected from prying eyes. Usually the
habitation is set apart by grillwork or fences or
handsomely-colored glass.

Near the church of San Sebastiano is a long
Fondamenta with a series of small palazzi
hiding gardens whose existence one would not
even suspect. One particular garden, now
owned by Jérôme Zieseniss, has a semicircular
wellhead in a paved area, with white table and
chairs close to the house. Dividing the paved
area from the rest of the garden are vases
overflowing with jasmine, lemon, azalea,
rhododendron and other flowers which change
every season. Two great pots of camellias guard
the *berceau* which is covered with vines and
wisteria. This *berceau* divides the garden into
two areas. On the right there is a long bed of
impatiens, a pomegranate, and a great cedar of
Lebanon. On the left, hidden by a wing of the
house, there are bushes of all colors along the
wall and in the middle of the lawn stands a
magnolia grandiflora with a double trunk. Two

*Sacerdoti garden.
'There is nothing that
has amazed me more in
this town built on the
water than to see the
number of beautiful
gardens it has'. Casola,*
Canon Pietro Casola's
Pilgrimage to Jerusalem
in the Year 1494, *p. 14.*

34

*Fullin garden.
A trompe-l'œil
structure to support
seasonal flowers.*

lines of stones bifurcate, one leading to another
wellhead covered with red geraniums, the other
to a secret gazebo, covered with roses, which
you reach by walking up four steps of Istrian
stone.

'There was a small courtyard, enclosed by
walls, and covered by a high trellis. Hanging
from the trellis, these were clusters of dark red
ripe grapes. Large pillars of wood supported
this living roof. A hook in one of these pillars
held the cage of a bird. There was a hole in this
roof of leaves large enough for a child to climb
through. The sun, shining through this roof,
silhouetted the lovely design of the grape-leaves
on the brick floor. In the small bower, half
room, half garden, with the smell of grapes and
the tepid air, the silence was so complete it was
possible to hear the sound the birds made, as
they hopped from one stick to another, without
even taking any notice of the entrance of
Andreas...' (H. VON HOFMANNSTHAL,
Andrea..., p. 82).

Near the Salute there is the most colorful
perfumed and 'living' ceiling in Venice. The
Barozzi garden was transformed by its owners
from an orchard into a room of roses. This
space is not large, but the unbelievable quantity
of flowers transforms it into something rich and
precious. This remarkable place is really an
extension of the house, where the family can
enjoy three seasons of the year. In the center of
the wall there is an amusing ancient mask that

has a faucet with a red hose dangling from its
mouth. The wall is covered with innumerable
antique family crests. This natural room ends in
a thick curtain of foliage though which one can
catch glimpses of the bell-towers and cupolas of
the Salute church.

'It was her refuge, the secret place of her
solitude, where her melancholy was protected
by the silent guards of her hiding place.
She was surrounded by the old, as well as the
new, ghosts of her melancholy thoughts'
(G. D'ANNUNZIO, *Il fuoco*, p. 355).

In the area of Santa Croce along the
Fondamenta del Gaffaro, hidden among many
other gardens, which are separated by walls,
there is a small green space which is the most
secret of the secret gardens of Venice. The
entrance hall of the palazzo opens onto a
narrow rectangular space which is enriched by
Boston vine mixed with different forms of ivy
which frame the doors and the windows. Along
the sides there are tiny red begonia and ferns.
In the center there is a wellhead formed by an
ancient Greek Corinthian capital that came
from the Orient. We are surprised to see, rising
from the center of this column, a hundred-year-
old *cycas palmata*, surrounded by a garland of
ancient boxwood. Leading to the garden there
is an iron gate inserted in an archway, beside
which there are two niches containing *putti*. We
then enter a grotto formed by rambling *phicus
rapens* which leads us into the raised garden. A

The garden of Casa Frollo still corresponds to those drawn by Jacopo de' Barbari.

38

previous pages
The garden of the Seminary.
The dense greenery and silence invite one to meditation.

on the right
Calzavara garden.
'Some of the gardens are hidden carefully, you have to look for them in the meanders of the city with great care'.
De Régnier, Esquisses vénitiennes, *p. 10.*

well-tended lawn is traversed by a path with irregular slabs of white and pink marble. Four *putti*, which represent the four seasons, are perched atop columns. The garden is full of colorful plants and flowers, each one of which has a special meaning for the owner. Amphorae and archaeological fragments, together with a great variety of interesting and unusual flowers, are combined so as to give the garden a rare charm and sense of infinite depth.

The secrets of this garden are not at all unusual in Venice, which in itself is like a giant jigsaw puzzle.

CONFIDENCES. The atmosphere of the Venetian garden creates a special intimacy between the people that share these special places – and often there can be only two such people. The ambiguity between things said and left unsaid is heightened by the atmosphere of the garden:

'This evening – I answered, – I will come and take a sorbet in your garden and please myself with viewing the jewelled pomegranate, shining beneath the firmament...' (G. D'ANNUNZIO, *Il fuoco,* p. 33).

Or: 'Leave with the others – then return... I shall await you at the Gradenigo gate' (G. D'ANNUNZIO, *Il fuoco,* p. 201).

Secret tales, revealed in hushed voices, a decadent atmosphere, long pauses...

'The gravel was heard grating underfoot, then, once again, a long silence. An indistinct noise came from the distant canals. The jasmine suddenly seemed to produce a stronger fragrance, like a heart beating faster' (G. D'ANNUNZIO, *Il fuoco,* p. 193).

These are examples of a complicit and confidential intimacy. Stories of passion, probably stronger in imagination than in reality, are still whispered today. The legend of the city that protects lovers and creates romantic situations is still alive.

The charmingly arranged semi-circular benches in many Venetian gardens bring to mind those romantic encounters of the past and allow us, even today, to savor the intimacy, the private trysts, the confidences, and the complicities of the past.

At Santa Caterina, in Cannaregio, where once stood the Palazzo Molin, demolished in 1819, there is now a garden created by an Englishwoman. It is interesting to know that the destroyed palace was once graced with a plaque recording the visit of Frederick IV, king of Denmark, who visited in 1709. Cleverly, the creator of the garden used the remaining pieces of marble from the cornices of the windows to outline the flowerbeds. The entrance to the garden from the canal is through the archway, which was once the main entrance. The English woman who, with her husband, started to recreate the garden in 1983, found there only a magnolia tree, a persimmon tree, and the iron skeleton of the ubiquitous *berceau*. Within five

*Ca' Zenobio.
A society based on
self-glorification had
to create gardens
of great splendor.*

42

previous pages
*The largest gardens
are situated on the
outskirts of the town
and on the Giudecca.*

years the Bellinato family created a delightful garden. Entering from Calle Racchetta, on the left we find a wellhead beautifully decorated with curving acanthus leaves and mythological characters. Lilies of the valley overflow from the top of the wellhead. The garden is divided in two parts by this beautiful feature, with the paved area near the house, and the rest covered with pebbles. In the flowerbeds along the wall there are multitudes of early spring flowers, such as narcissus and tulips, as well as bushes and trees which grow well in the shade. On a rock in the center of a small round pool filled with nymphs stands a *putto*. The walls all around are covered with honeysuckle, wisteria, bignonia, Boston and various other kinds of ivy, while in contrast the *berceau* is covered with small white eighteenth-century roses. Two palm trees (*chamaerops excelsa*) are protected by brick edgings. At the bottom of the garden, two benches and a table invite one to rest. As in the old days, the garden is looked after by the owners themselves.

There is another interesting garden on the Zattere along the Fondamenta delle Toreselle, which is also divided into small spaces. There is a charming long house that runs along the Giudecca canal, protected by a high wall of brick and Istrian stone. All along the top of the wall there is a series of most delightful *putti*. Once just one garden surrounded the villa, which is still the property of the Rocca family, but it has now been divided into a series of delightful small gardens connected by a walkway.

We enter through a small passageway, and we can choose which of the four gardens now surrounding the villa we wish to enter. One of the most delightful is the garden at the corner, which still shows signs of splendor and taste. There is an elegantly worked balustrade upon which rambling roses decorate an Art Nouveau bas-relief: a languid lady lying on a cushion of roses. The great olive trees, brought from the Greek islands, spill over the top of the walls framing the cupola of Palladio's church of the Redentore. Statues, angels, columns, and capitals, brought from their villa on the Brenta river, decorate the lawn in the English style. A variety of ornamental flowers add color and harmony to this charming spot.

Gabriele D'Annunzio, Isidora Duncan, Eleonora Duse, and the Marchesa Luisa Casati Stampa are among a few of the great names that still reverberate as we contemplate the beauty of this garden and we are reminded of the time when the quest for pure beauty through the senses was an absolute value. The love that could not be spoken; the secret *amours* which challenged the public morality of the time; the furtive loving and longing – all this comes to mind...

'From the first hour of darkness, Stelio would hurry to the house of his beloved, entering through the great gate of the Gradenigo garden, walking through the trees and bushes that had returned to their wild state. The Foscarina had managed to extend her garden through one of the neighboring palaces through a breach in the neighboring wall' (G. D'ANNUNZIO, *Il fuoco*, p. 318).

The tiniest space in the secret gardens of Venice provides a sense of time, place and occasion, thus giving us a sense of intrigue, of mystery, of fugitive thoughts and feelings which defy classification. Despite the many changes of ownership and the different form that each owner imposed on the garden, these silent spaces seem to have taken on a life of their own.

The tiny garden of D'Annunzio on the Grand Canal attempts to hide itself from the curious eyes of the passers-by on the water. A portico covered with dense vine covers the low wall on the canal. There is a lawn in front of the red house, and a huge wisteria makes it difficult even to open the side door to the garden. On the left there is a fountain. Everything in the garden has been carefully measured and ordered. Very little trace remains of the spirit of D'Annunzio, except perhaps a unusual door-bell: a little angel with fiery eyes looks out to surprise and disturb the visitor.

In Venice the relationship with nature is different from that in any other city. One feels the separation from the earth very strongly. Water is Nature, but also acts as a barrier that can only be crossed by artificial means. The landscape on the horizon is that of the flat sea.

In the Venetian garden the eye never roves towards sinuous lines beyond the trees and bushes. The end of the garden is always a surrounding wall or the mirror of the water.

Within the green world of the garden, space is broken up into ever smaller areas, in a search for personal expression. The habit of looking at things close-at-hand focuses our attention on passions, sentiments, and every nuance of our changing moods.

Each garden has its own distinct personality and with this in mind, Henry James assigned to a Venetian garden the role of a protagonist in his novel, *The Aspern Papers*. In the novel, the

Barozzi garden. Even today elements of the Renaissance garden still play a functional role.

43

*Palazzo Minotto.
'It is this garden which
has first taken your
heart, with a glimpse
caught through the
great open door of the
palace'. Howells,*
Venetian Life, *p. 87.*

*on the right
Decorative elements in
highly secret gardens,
such as this one near the
Architectural Institute.*

*overleaf
Sacerdoti garden on
the Giudecca.
Semicircular benches
in stone are
particularly favoured
in Venetian gardens.*

garden itself is the indispensable instrument allowing access to possession of the secrets of *The Aspern Papers*.

'This, however, didn't prevent my gratification from being great as I became aware on reaching the end of the garden that my younger *padrona* was seated in one of the bowers. At first I made out but an indistinct figure, not in the least counting on such an overture from one of my hostesses; it even occurred to me that some enamoured maid-servant had stolen in to keep a tryst with her sweetheart. I was going to turn away, not to frighten her, when the figure rose to its height and I recognised Miss Bordereau's niece. I must do myself the justice that I didn't wish to frighten her either, and much as I had longed for some such accident I should have been capable of retreating. It was as if I had laid a trap for her by coming home earlier than usual and by adding to that oddity my invasion of the garden' (H. JAMES, *The Aspern Papers*, p. 80).

The stranger in search of *The Aspern Papers* prepares a trap made of flowers and plants. 'It's absurd if you like, for a man, but I can't live without flowers – ... She came nearer, as if, though she mistrusted me, I had drawn her by an invisible thread. I went on again, and she continued as she followed me: – We've a few, but they're very common. It costs too much to cultivate them; one has to have a man –. – Why shouldn't I be the man? – I asked – I'll work

without wages; or rather I'll put in a gardener. You shall have the sweetest flowers in Venice'(H. JAMES, *The Aspern Papers,* p. 56).

The garden that Henry James describes still exists today. The Palazzo Cappello and its garden are even more dilapidated now than they were at the turn of the century. There are many moss-covered statues which help to create a melancholy mood. Some still stand on their pillars, some are fixed in the earth, and some are lying on the ground, like wounded and long-forgotten heroes.

'Seen from above the garden was in truth shabby, yet I felt at a glance that it had great capabilities' (H. JAMES, *The Aspern Papers*, p. 57).

In the novel the garden becomes the means whereby the cheat insinuates himself into the confidences of the innocent but withdrawn heroines.

'I made a point of spending as much time as possible in the garden, to justify the picture I had originally given of my horticultural passion... As soon as I had got my rooms arranged and could give the question proper thought I surveyed the place with a clever expert and made terms for having it put in order. I was sorry to do this, for personally I liked it better as it was, with its weeds and its wild rich tangle, its sweet characteristic Venetian shabbiness... I would batter the old women with lilies – I would bombard their

Renato Levi-Morenos garden.
'The alternate ebb and flow of the tide changes the look of the place, sometimes land, and sometimes islands, and your houses are like those of water-fowl..., for the land is secured only by osiers and wattle... and in place of horses you keep boats tied up in front of your homes'. Cassiodorus, 538 b.C.

on the right
Former Palazzo Contarini on the Grand Canal.

overleaf
Rocca garden.
'As I went by the gate of the... little garden, the flowers saluted me with a breath of perfume – I think the white honeysuckle was first to offer me this politeness – and the dumpy little statues looked far more engaging than usual'. Howells, Venetian Life, *p. 124.*

citadel with roses. Their door would have to yield to the pressure when a mound of fragrance should be heaped against it. The place in truth had been brutally neglected. The Venetian capacity for dawdling is of the largest, and for a good many days unlimited litter was all my gardener had to show for his ministrations. There was a great digging of holes and carting about of earth, and after a while I grew so impatient that I had thoughts of sending for my bouquets to the nearest stand... finally, though the delay was long, [I] perceived some appearances of bloom. This encouraged me and I waited serenely enough till they multiplied. Meanwhile the real summer days arrived and began to pass, and as I look back upon them they seem to me almost the happiest of my life. I took more and more care to be in the garden whenever it was not too hot. I had an arbour arranged and a low table and an armchair put into it; and I carried out books and portfolios – (I had always some business of writing in hand) – and worked and waited and mused and hoped, while the golden hours elapsed and the plants drank in the light and the inscrutable old palace turned pale and then, as the day waned, began to recover and flush and my papers rustled in the wandering breeze of the Adriatic...' (H. JAMES, *The Aspern Papers*, p. 74).

This passage shows us that the writer understood how Venice is so fragmented an entity that only an enigmatic and oblique approach could permit him to penetrate its hostile texture, and achieve his difficult, if not impossible aims. Even today the barriers constituted by circumlocutions, by carefully manipulated phrases, or by gates and walls protected with glass shards, grills and multicolored screens, all recall the implicit contradiction on which Venetian life is founded. The doors are closed to the passer-by. But for those who live there, the internal space becomes a place to share; although access is limited to few people, all those who look onto the garden share in the transformations of nature. It is another version of the communal life of the Campo, with its vociferous inhabitants who carry the colors of the garden onto their own balconies, thus recalling the complex origins of the city.

The idea of flight is inherent to Venice: things are hidden, knowledge is never flaunted but masked. In no other city is the garden such an element of complicity, an excuse to arrive at one's goal via winding roads, alluding to a world that can only be intuited but never grasped. Like an Islamic city, Venice is beyond analysis or easy classification. While it is easy to see the surface and observe the beautiful facades, such as the glorious decorations, the marvelous mosaics of gold, the inhabitants still maintain secrets which the western world will never fathom.

Rites of Celebration

EALS. '... the gardens of Venice would deserve a page to themselves. They are infinitely more numerous than the arriving stranger can suppose; they nestle with a charm all their own in the complications of most back views. Some of them are exquisite, many are large, and even the scrappiest have an artful understanding, in the interest of color, with the waterways that edge their foundations. On the small canals, in the hunt of amusement, they are the prettiest surprise of all. The tangle of plants and flowers crowds over the battered walls, the greenness makes an arrangement with the rosy sordid brick...' (H. JAMES, *Italian Hours*, p. 43).

From the *piano nobile* of certain palaces, in the warm season, it is possible to see geometrically designed flowerbeds, full of vivid colors, that recall the arabesque designs of Oriental carpets, which have been in use in Venice since the twelfth century at least. Ever since ancient times plants and flowers have provided a simple system of symbolism to identify power and those who wield it:
'Now I will sing to my well-beloved a song of my beloved touching his vineyard.
My well-beloved hath a vineyard in a very fruitful hill. And he fenced it, and gathered out the stones thereof, and planted it with the choicest vines, and built a tower in the midst of it, and also made a winepress therein...' (ISAIAH 5: 1-2).

In another passage in the Bible we can find an even more elementary explanation of the connection between nature, symbols and power: 'Thy mother is like a vine in thy blood, planted by the waters: she was fruitful and full of branches by reason of many waters. And she had strong rods for the sceptres of them that bare rule...' (EZECHIEL 19: 10-11).

Seals are important images: not just names, not just words, not just definitions; seals serve as brands, as symbols, translating depth of meaning into images. Family crests very often consist of simple elements derived from nature, such as the rose, the acanthus-leaf, branches of certain trees; in other cases, as with the *Scuole* (guilds of people with the same skills, or with the same religious beliefs, or from the same country) they are allusive and hermetic, communicating messages that need to be deciphered and interpreted.

In the *Roman de la rose*, which is cited by all who write about gardens since it presents the structure of the medieval garden with its high protecting walls, the rose is an allegory of love. The poem speaks of that which cannot be explicitly stated, but only comprehended through the elaboration of fantastic images. A river flows through the garden, at the heart of which stands a rose-bush, protected by

'On the Giudecca the garden of the Gritti is delicate and rare for its greenery, for its buildings, and for sculptures and paintings. On this island other noble gardens are those of Andrea Dandolo on the point opposite San Giorgio Maggiore and those of the Mocenigo, the Vendramini and the Cornaro, and many others that are scattered over this island with extraordinary beauty and delicacy'.
Sansovino, Venetia città nobilissima..., *p. 369.*

*Palazzo Balbi Valier.
The sun and the moon
on the pavement of
the inner courtyard.
The decoration
of the gratings is
perhaps linked to
astrology and more
simply to the idea that
rainwater was welcome.*

surrounding briars. The symbolic systems of the sacred and the profane are intricately intertwined, each bearing upon the other in a series of images which become poetic in their very ambiguity. The rose is the symbol of Woman in general and of the Madonna in particular. The Mystical Rose in the Litany of the Virgin is, in the *Roman de la Rose*, the mysterious tabernacle of the Garden of Love and of the Cavalier.

There is no shortage of roses in Venetian gardens. Every kind of rose-bush, common or rare, cultivated or wild, can be found there. The rose bushes may be formed as trees or bred as ramblers; frequently they twine around *berceaux* and pergolas.

Another symbol frequently found in classical and medieval art and architecture is the acanthus leaf, which ornamented Corinthian columns, funereal carriages, the robes of famous men, of architects or victorious heroes.

In Venice the seals of the *Scuole*, the Confraternities and the noble families are to be found throughout the city. Examples are the five-leafed rose of the Donà dalle Rose, sculpted on various wellheads and coats-of-arms; the scorpions on the iron gates of the Palazzo Brandolin; and the emblematic stone sun and moon faces used as gratings in the courtyard of Palazzo Balbi Valier.

The activities and the conditions of any society at a given moment of time lead to the use of signs, symbols, means of communication which represent the interests and concerns of the moment. In Venice, many of the 'noble' families and the *Scuole* created crests and symbols, usually incircled, suggesting the influence of Byzantium. From the Orient, Venetians often brought back *patere* in marble

or other stones, which contained abstract designs, portraits of Emperors and heroes, birds, animals, and flowers. These elements were placed in the walls of gardens, palaces or homes. Within the circles, one finds signs of the history and experience of these families and *Scuole*, as well as preferred symbols, meaningful to them, although not always understood centuries later.

SELF-REPRESENTATION. The Venetians were not innocent of self-aggrandizement and conspicuous display. Palaces were often ornamented, internally and externally, with plaques testifying to the passage of great personages. The gardens of the great palaces, such as those on the Grand Canal, also contributed to this display of family importance, with rare flowers, plants and trees, arranged according to meticulous rules.

The gardens of Venice have a complex history and tend to follow a well-defined style. They were often sub-divided into flowerbeds with elaborate patterns and fountains in the form of ancient bowls or vases. *Berceaux*, pathways, and pergolas were also part of the overall plan. While the *pergola* is rectangular, the *berceau* is round and is not merely decorative in function, providing protection from the humid summer air. The *berceau* has a long history, and has been found in the tombs of the noble Nacht (1425 b.C.) and Sen-Nefer (1435 b.C.), both in Thebes. In both tombs, the vaults are covered with frescoes representing vine branches. In Venice, particularly beautiful *berceaux* are those in the Zieseniss garden near San Sebastiano, and the Ca' Leon and Gozzi gardens on the Giudecca.

Titian had a garden on the lagoon, at San Canciano. He used to invite his friends there

*In the gardens of
Venice exotic and
luxurious features are
often found, recalling
those journeys to
distant lands where
nature and fables
were so different.*

and spent much time cultivating it.

'The Abbot Cadorin reports that Titian lived in a house nearby, rented from Leonardo Molin. In 1549 he took... an empty lot alongside it from Molin's widow Bianca and transformed it into a beautiful garden where he enjoyed entertaining his friends. The Rector Priscicane, in a footnote to his *6 Libri della Lengua Latina*, printed in 1553, writes that he was invited with Aretino, Sansovino and Jacopo Nardi by Titian to spend the mid-August holiday in this garden – which was at the extreme part of Venice on the sea, where you can see the lovely island of Murano, and other beautiful scenery – ... In our days the house was subjected to rebuilding, during which the tree with the round leaves that Titan painted in the *Martyrdom of St. Peter* was uprooted. Since then the Fondamenta Nuove have been created and you can see the lagoon only through the narrow Calle Colombina' (G. TASSINI, *Curiosità veneziane...*, p. 682).

The city is continuously in a state of flux. Statues, with their aura of permanence, serve as the most frequent means of ornamentation in the gardens. They testify most clearly to wealth and prestige – yesterday as today.

The statues were often intended to impress visitors, leaving them speechless with awe and amazement. In the open spaces they do not merely serve a decorative function, but have allusive meanings. They are often situated in niches between sumptuous colonnades. The Brandolin garden, behind Palazzo Giustinian, has unique features. A large door on a narrow Calle is guarded, on the inside, by two reclining statues, on curved brick walls, between oleander trees, with a backdrop of variegated ivy which covers the whole wall. The area in front of the house is paved, with a wellhead in the center. The building itself has an ancient wisteria. Two stairways, one of five steps, and another of seven steps, lead to the main part of the garden. The seven steps lead up to a vine-shaded gazebo. The other stairway, crowned by two half-nude caryatids with huge moustaches, leads into a *parterre* garden in which the limited space is multiplied by narrow paths of concentric boxwood arranged in the shape of a heart.

The most exhaustive and surprising description of an exceptional garden that has since disappeared is provided by Martinoni: '... on the only spot on the Grand Canal that has a Fondamenta on each side, there was the Palazzo of Count Gerolamo Cavazza' (F. SANSOVINO, *Venetia città nobilissima...*, p. 393).

Martinoni considered this garden as one of the richest and most remarkable in the city. He devotes particular attention to the ground-floor, which the Count had transformed into an area of delight, using areas that were usually given over to purely utilitarian functions.

'The gallery is decorated with five different

*Gozzi garden on the
Giudecca.
The* berceau, *unlike
the rectangular* pergola,
has a round shape.

on the right
*Statue in the Gozzi
garden.*

overleaf
*In the Cosulich garden
at San Sebastiano
the decorative and
architectural elements
dominate and
confine the greenery.*

levels of ornamentation. Whoever enters is
awe-struck by the height and light of the white
ceiling, and by the festoons, figures and other
ornaments in stucco... the painted
perspectives... on the right and left of the niches
there are statues, and between them
medallions, heads and busts' – and Martinoni
continues with elaborate descriptions of the
five orders of decoration:
'In a large niche on the right there is a huge
statue of Neptune with a dolphin at his feet,
and a marble lion on each side of him.
Emerging from the gallery, towards the left,
there is an eight-sided wellhead of Verona
stone, surrounded by vases filled with myrtle –
the plant of Venus –. There are two stairways,
converging toward the top, forming a grotto
decorated in an elaborate manner, with
Capami, Giazuoli, sea-shells, of so many shapes
and colors, that delight the eye, by the skill with
which they are arranged, and by the shapes and
figures they form; in front of the figure of
Neptune is another grotto, completely covered
in mother-of-pearl...'
 Further on, in the empty space of a door,
there were four huge mirrors, framed in gold,
multiplying and expanding the space.
Martinoni claims that this use of mirrors was an
invention of the Count, which was then copied
by other Venetian nobles.
'This area then proceeds to a loggia, with
columns, frames and pillars of Verona marble,

with a stucco ceiling and gouache paintings all
around; but above these are placed paintings of
birds, flowers, and hunting scenes, inlaid with
lapis lazuli and other precious stones, in the
Florentine style. There is also a beautiful table
made with the same technique... From this
loggia, through huge windows, you see a low
court, with perspective paintings by Brescian
artists; there are large orange trees with beautiful
thick bright foliage, in spite of the fact that they
do not get much sun. There are three beautifully
inlaid doors, leading to the last room, with a
vaulted stone ceiling, divided into
compartments and decorated with stucco; the
rest of the room is similarly decorated, with
fluted columns, with five niches furnished with
statues; and two large paintings; one with Diana
bathing; and another with Andromeda in
chains, the sea-monster and Perseus flying down
to save her, painted by the Cavalier Cairo
Milanese... I will not speak of the vases with
flowers and other beautiful objects that leave no
corner unadorned, in order not to lengthen this
account, which has of necessity been an
extensive one. It is the only ground-floor
apartment in Venice that is so splendidly
decorated and beautifully furnished that one
would feel at ease entertaining the most exalted
guests there – and it had the virtue of being cool
in summer and almost warm in winter...'
 The architectural quality of the Italian
garden was perfectly suited to Venice and thus

*From the Giudecca
this garden opens
towards the canal and
Bacino of San Marco.*

62

*The Lucheschi garden at
San Barnaba has wide
symmetrical flowerbeds.*

the style lasted longer there than elsewhere. Such gardens answer the need to contain the symbols of self-celebration within a limited space, a typically Venetian concern.

Often Venetian gardens are small in size and, owing to a rigorous symmetry, can be surveyed in their entirety from any point. In the seventeenth century gardens became more elaborate. Theatrical devices were employed to make the space look larger than it really was. Every corner had to be different, in an attempt to astound and impress observers.

Formal rules concerning the location and arrangement of plants and flowers became codified, in order to increase the elegance and prestige of the palazzi. The foremost promulgator in the Veneto of this kind of codification was Paolo Bartolomeo Clarici, whose treatise was published after his death in 1726.

'The first principle in creating a worthy garden is to plan the appropriate partitions, separations and compartmentations of the entire area. When such order is lacking, there will be no ordered prospect, which is what is required to bring out the beauty of the flowers and plants. Since some of these must be placed in vases, while others must be placed in earth, one must therefore form, either from grassy earth or painted wood, four small platforms or pyramids, situated at each corner of the compass, in order to place the vases in the correct spot and climate required by the nature of the plant or flower; certain planks and unsightly staircases must be avoided, which give the place a vulgar, rustic appearance. The ground shall be laid out in flowerbeds which must be well-ordered and divided into beautiful figures, making sure that the flowers on long stalks are placed at the furthest point in the garden so that they do not cover and conceal the smaller ones. And these must be placed in flowerbeds in proportion to their quality and should always be arranged so that there is easy access for proper care and watering; these beds should be four feet wide and six feet long at most, and there should be two feet between them. Some people surround the flowerbeds with *Pianchette* others use Boxwood whose evergreen seems essential to bring out the beauty of the Garden. The worst would be to surround them with Thyme, or Marjoram or Sage, or other strong-smelling herbs, some of which are short-lived; since they rebud at different times, they would destroy all the beautiful order of the Garden, whose greatest

Ca' Dolfin.
The water was collected
in the wells. There were
two systems: artesian
wells and cisterns that
filtered the rainwater
from the gratings.

64

on the right
Peggy Guggenheim
garden.
From above
unexpected green areas
can be seen. They are
the most secret and
inaccessible gardens.

overleaf
Venetian gardens are
not only hidden among
the houses, but there
are very few actually on
the Grand Canal, like
this one belonging to
Ca' Vendramin Calergi.

beauty lies in the perfection of its symmetry, without which, however lovely the flowers, there can be no beauty; this was a failing of the ancient Gardens, where the confusion of the design, and of the plants and flowers themselves, spoilt the pattern and prestige' (P.B. CLARICI, *Istoria e coltura...*, p. 4).

Clarici's dictates can still be recognised today in some gardens, such as that of Palazzo Bernardo, now belonging to Countess Maria Lucheschi near San Barnaba, on the Grand Canal. The garden has large, wide symmetrical beds framed with dwarf boxwood, and cultivated with roses of all different colors. The pattern consists of three circles, each one separately framed with boxwood, and the whole contained within a large lawned rectangle. The largest round bed contains the tallest palm-tree in Venice. The garden rises at the far end to a thick curtain of trees that act as a stage-backdrop, concealing another building. Along the walls there are bushes of all varieties, in different shades of green. We can see a certain ludic tendency here, in the topiary work, the search for strange and exotic plants and the *giochi d'acqua*.

In the eighteenth century tastes changed in the direction of ever greater playfulness. Gardens became full of sham curtains and stages, carefully carved bushes, grotesque figures, statues, *casini* for gambling and cultivated conversation, libraries. An example

of this type of garden is the one at Ca' Zenobio, near the Carmini. Built by Gaspari, the palazzo has an unusual form for Venice, with two wings projecting into the garden. There is a print by Luca Carlevarijs that shows the *parterre* of this garden, designed like a beautifully-patterned floor in multi-colored marble, although actually made of plants, flowers, boxwood, pebbles and vases. On either side, protected by high walls, stands an array of ancient statues. An elegant gate links the two wings, separating the courtyard from the garden. The gate, courtyard and palace still exist today. The garden has now entirely changed. Where there was once an elaborate floral arabesque, we now find tables, chairs, cherubs, and a multitude of *pistosforo* bushes. At a later date (1767) a library, by Temanza, was constructed at the end of the garden, closing it off.

The casino of Palazzo Zane, in Rio Marin, also created by Gaspari in the eighteenth century, serves as a backdrop to the garden. Again we can see the garden in a print by Carlevarijs. It is rigorously geometrical in its design, divided into rectangles with square flowerbeds and statues placed symmetrically at the center of the beds. There is no vegetation but the two gardeners, one with a wheelbarrow and the other bending to the ground, suggest the garden is being prepared. On the right a border of stones forms a long raised flowerbed; along the wall a trellis supports the climbing plants.

*Carlevarijs' prints
show the parterre of
the garden, arranged
around floral patterns,
and reveals the
geometrical precision
of gardens at the time.*

*Ca' Tron.
In some cases the old
practice of dividing
the garden into
public and private
zones has been kept up.*

There are two huge dogs in the background. Two gentlemen are in the center foreground, as if discussing the plan.

If we pass from Carlevarijs' prints to the scenery of the Grand Canal, we can see how self-promotion was a constant concern in Venice. Two different kinds of garden survive on the Grand Canal: the formal ones, and the wilder ones, overtaken by Nature. The former attempt to maintain some of the rigor of the seventeenth and eighteenth century, while the latter give the illusion of unrestrained Nature, although in reality they are always under the strict control of the gardener.

Coming from the Bacino (the wide open space in front of San Marco) and moving up the Grand Canal, we find, on the left, a low white structure, the first level of a never-completed palazzo, once known as dei Leoni, but now famous as the former residence of Peggy Guggenheim, and home to the Guggenheim Collection. An avalanche of green pours over the front of the building, revealing the existence of the garden behind. There is an ornamental gate which separates the grounds of the palazzo from the Grand Canal. Through this gate, from the water, one can see the statue of the *Angel of the City*, by Marino Marini. Behind the palazzo, there is a paved area, in lozenge forms, with a large stone throne, a gazebo with greenery, stone benches where one can enjoy the shade and sit, chat, and contemplate the sculptures of Giacometti, Arp,

Moore, Armitage, Paolozzi, De Kooning, Ernst, Gonzalez and others. These sculptures are a modern example of decoration as self-promotion. Surrounding all this we find terracotta urns filled with white marguerites and petunias and cherubs, decorating the rest of the terrace.

Farther on, at San Vio, at the Palazzo Balbi Valier, the arch of the gate frames four symmetrical beds of red roses. Near the water, spring is announced each year by a Judas tree with its violet petals. The great chestnut tree shades a paved area. Oleander, Virginia creeper, jasmine, and ivy crown the walls and also climb up to the loggia of the Palazzo Polignac, which overlooks this garden. Toward this wall there is a basin filled with water lilies. Orchids also grow in this garden, their microclimate made possible since a screen of *pitosforo* protects them from harsh weather. Behind a low wall, up three steps, there is a tiny secret garden of great delight with azaleas, hortensia, peonies, forsythia, ancient roses, and, at the proper time, narcissus, daffodils, and iris.

The Levi-Morenos garden, opposite Ca' Corner della Regina at San Stae, is an example of a more natural garden. Wild it is not, but it nonetheless gives a feeling of freedom and easiness. A rich iron balustrade protects a circular stairway which leads to the only *belvedere* on the Grand Canal. In 1914, E.V. Lucas wrote about this garden in his book

*Renato Levi-Morenos
garden on the Grand
Canal.
Between 1600 and 1800
there were more
botanical gardens in
Venice alone than in
all the rest of Italy.*

70

*Garden of the former
Palazzo Morosini 'del
Giardin'.
A concrete staircase
covered in wisteria leads
into an area cultivated
as a vegetable garden.*

A Wanderer in Venice and even then he noted how unusual a garden it is: 'Then a nice house with a tumbled garden, and in spring purple wisteria and red Judas-trees, and then the Rio San Felice...'

Going on toward the railway station, further up the Grand Canal, we find what is probably the most historical of the gardens of Venice. Martinoni speaks of the Grimani garden (today the Vendramin-Calergi), well-known for the rarity of its plants, and the exceptional quality of the site, being 'situated directly on the Grand Canal'.

ORNAMENTS. Venetians never fail to embellish and enrich those parts of their homes that are 'on view', rooms or areas that may not have been used regularly but which served as show-pieces. Nature, flowers, and trees are treated as ornaments too. Gardens are full of ornaments, whether they be statues or special varieties of roses. The garden itself could be considered the ornament of the house, giving it color and freshness, and absorbing or refracting the light according to the season. The greenery that hangs over balustrades, walls, and gates enlivens simple homes as well as great palazzi.

Once in Venice there were also roof gardens. Martinoni talks of one of these gardens in the house of Simon Santo at San Gregorio, who had constructed a landscape with his own hands: a structure built on a wide terrace. He

had created open spaces that simulated a stream and artificial mountains. We can imagine the difficulties, in the the past, of making a roof impermeable, and bringing water up to a high level. Not only was it a difficult engineering task, but incredibly expensive to achieve. No obstacle stands in the way of Venetians when they are eager to enhance their homes and gardens and enjoy their pleasures. A modern example of a roof-garden is the one created by Alberta Foscari on the roof of an eighteenth-century house in Campo San Maurizio, with a lawn, geraniums, climbing roses, ivy and oleander.

The Morosini family, in their palazzo at Santi Apostoli, created such a marvellous garden that they gained the nickname, 'del Giardin'. Today, the famous garden no longer exists. In its place there is a retirement home for old women run by Dominican nuns. Where once stood the palazzo, there is now an open space, half-garden, half-orchard, and the former area of the garden is now occupied by a building. The Palladian palazzetto that flanked the canal has been substituted by a garden, partly given over to vegetables. The entrance door at the water's edge is of noble proportions, and is possibly a remnant of the original water entrance to the building. From Calle Valmarana, the land entrance is through a vestibule, after which you reach a round *berceau* covered with white roses and honeysuckle,

'Since I received your
kind note I have been
awaiting the propitious
moment and light to
go and have a glance,
a further glance at the
little house with the
garden on the Grand
Canal, to the right of
Palazzo Guggenheim'.
James, Letters, 1907.

72

which leads to a grotto filled with white roses
and containing a figure of the Virgin Mary. To
the right of the *berceau*, there are vegetable
beds. On the left, the structure (where once the
original garden lay) has two rusticated windows
that seem to have come from the original
building. In the sun, protected by a wall, there
is a long, narrow bed of fragrant herbs, such as
rosemary, sage, marjoram, many varieties of
thyme, and a carpet of dwarf parsley. At the end
of this building there is a fine stairway – albeit
made of concrete – shaded by wisteria, which
leads to a square area filled with tomatoes.
Pergolas of vines protect the passageways, and
hide the tools. In the center of a round bed of
daisies there is an incredible white angel, which
seems to fly out of the flowerbed.

Considerable powers of imagination are
required to reconstruct the fabulous Morosini
garden. Writers throughout the ages described
it as extraordinary. The garden of the 'Morosini
del Giardin' was delimited by a long and
narrow rectangular building of the sixteenth
century, the Casino of the Palazzo overlooking
the Rio San Canciano, and by a much larger
seventeenth-century building, overlooking
Calle Valmarana. The first writer to mention
the garden was Francesco Sansovino, in the
sixteenth century. He starts the lists of Venetian
gardens with this one, saying that it was the
perfect realization of the ideal garden, due to
the rarity and variety of the plants therein, as

much as to the beauty of the architecture,
sculpture and paintings. Ridolfi, in 1648, in his
Life of Paolo Veronese, refers to the fact that the
artist had painted, for Francesco Erizzo, first
owner of the palazzo, frescoes of ancient
architecture, and scenes of classical landscapes,
in the portico. Ridolfi attributes the
architecture to Palladio. He attributed to
Veronese a stucco statue of Mars, and he was
certain that the other statues were by
Alessandro Vittoria. He also says that the
palazzo was already owned by the Morosini
family. In 1660, Marco Boschini, in his *Carta del
navegar pitoresco*, was so intrigued by a natural
sculpture in the garden – a walnut root that
resembled a many-headed monster – that he
called it a masterpiece. 'In Ca' Morosini in
Patriarcado, the roots of a walnut tree have been
incised by nature into varied forms and appear
to be strange heads. The natural 'spots', placed
there by Nature, assume many colors, which
Man could not duplicate with a paintbrush.Of
course, they are just 'spots', but, believe it or
not, their bizarreness is so amazing, they
become beautifully galant'.

Cicogna, complaining about the general
decline of the area, in his journal entry of 21
April 1829, reports that some ancient statues
from the Morosini garden at San Canciano
were moved to the Morosini-Gattemburg
Palazzo at Santo Stefano. He was also disturbed
by the way the Palladian architecture was falling

*Peggy Guggenheim
garden.
'And here at the end of
the Campiello...
statues... on whose
limbs the dry branches
of the ivy looked
like veins in relief'.
D'Annunzio,*
Il fuoco, *p. 318.*

73

apart. Perhaps the beautiful barrier-gate used as a window may be the only remaining structure from the building that Ridolfi attributed to Palladio.

Talking about gardens considered as ornaments of the palazzo, Martinoni provides brief descriptions which are more like a list than anything else:
'The garden of Savorgnan is large and delightful; the Sorian has unusual plants; at la Croce the garden of Secretario Businelli is unique; and Pietro Zaghis' is planted with rare flowers, including some from China and far away places. At the Carmini there is that of Luigi Foscarini, Procurator of San Marco, that of the Donati, of Monsignor Cornaro, Bishop of Padua. At the garden of Agostino Barbarigo at the Angelo Raffaele, there is a plaque with gilded letters which records the visit of Maximilian II, king of Poland, in 1592...' (F. SANSOVINO, *Venetia città nobilissima*..., p. 369).

It was the age of Arcimboldo's extraordinary paintings, of marvellous scientific discoveries, and of obsessive studies into deformed shapes of humans, animals and other objects. Martinoni also refers to the fact that Titian, who lived nearby, painted a fresco of Hercules on the door, which he considers to be one of his earliest works. He states that part of the garden was transformed into a courtyard paved with patterned bricks and subdivided by strips of white marble.

Often palazzi and houses take Nature as a decorative pattern. Nature is imitated not only in the architectural structure but also in the decorative details of the silk or stone, in the paintings on the interior of the walls that flank the garden. In this way the atmosphere of the garden is brought into the house. Thus there is a continuous dialogue or interchange between the various ornamental elements: for example, *berceaux* of roses, climbing ivy and cypresses are often designed and planned in the same fashion as the statues and the gazebos. The Battistello garden near the Carmini is a low, wide rectangle, protected by walls toward Calle Ragusei, which separates it from what remains of the Foscarini garden. Near the house there is a paved area with a large rectangular marble table. The entire space is covered by a *berceau* draped with vines. On the wall on the right there is a vase with sunflowers carved in stone.

Natural objects are imitated in stone, concrete or wrought-iron. What is this yearning that drives people to decorate a garden with a stone vase full of flowers that will never fade? The undying beauty of the unopened bud serves to demonstrate that Man, with his works, can accomplish what Nature cannot... Naked or half-naked figures of men and women greet the visitors with their dramatic but unchanging poses.

The garden of Palazzo Cappello-Malipiero overlooks the Grand Canal at San Samuele,

overleaf
*Palazzo Cappello.
Copies of Roman statues.*

Francesco Guardi,
Garden of Palazzo
Contarini dal Zaffo
alla Misericordia.
*Formerly it hosted
cultural gatherings.
It is now given over to
an old people's home.*

on the right
*Barnabò garden.
The recent restoration
of the balustrade and
the care with which the
garden is looked after
make it a fine example
of how a private garden
can be kept up.*

overleaf
*San Francesco della
Vigna: the vegetable
garden and the cloisters.*

protected by a balustrade in Istrian stone, covered with white roses. The present owners, the Barnabò family, gave the shape to this garden in the 1930s. Towards the canal, in the center of large symmetrical beds, bordered with boxwood and filled with roses, there is a Renaissance well with the crest and portrait of the young lady of the Cappello family who married a member of the Malipiero family. Eighteenth-century statues, probably the work of the sculptor Bonazza, originally for another garden in the country, add to the elegance of the place. On each side of the well, there is a female figure, looking toward the water. On the other side of the garden, there are statues of the four seasons, at the four corners of a fountain, where a cherub embraces a dolphin spouting water; facing this there is a large nymphaeum, with a statue of Neptune within, rising from a semi-circular basin. The iron gate, guarded by Antaeus and Hercules on one side, and Ganymede and Jupiter on the other, leads downs to a paved courtyard that acts as an extension of the entrance hall to the palazzo. This garden is a recent expression of Venetian taste, combining the decorative and the archaic. Greek and Roman heroes, mythological figures and gods, are clustered, in the relatively small spaces of Venetian gardens, to testify to the great status of the owners themselves.

The plants change throughout the year, and,

simultaneously, as the light and shadow alter, the decoration of the interior changes as well. Everything that is not stone is transformed by the passing of the seasons and the mutation of light.

'The afternoon declines; there's not a breath of air; the new leaves breathe and hope while the old leaves meditate and remember. A large flowering wisteria covers the entire wall, all the way up to the roof, starting from a twisted trunk, resembling a tangle of ropes' (G. D'ANNUNZIO, *Notturno*, p. 236).

Amid this frantic exchange of life and death, of nature and stone, D'Annunzio feels the contradiction implicit in the idea of nature as ornament:
'... with her childlike grace, Sirenetta takes my hand, leading me to a rose-bush on a long stem, and says, – Look at the rose! – The rose-bush and the girl seem to become one thing. As she holds the stem between two fingers, the little rose seems to have been born in her hand, like the beginning of a spring metamorphosis' (G. D'ANNUNZIO, *Notturno*, p. 234).

One of the few images of a garden we can recognize, in the etching of Guardi now in the Ashmolean Museum at Oxford, is an illustration of the garden of Contarini dal Zaffo alla Misericordia, done in 1780. The garden covers half of Guardi's page, leaving much space for the autumnal sky. On the left, the garden is framed by the Casino called *degli*

*Barnabò garden.
The most important
palazzi on the Grand
Canal have an entrance
hall that extends from
the ground or canal
door towards the
garden. The statues
at the entrance signal
the passing from
inside to outside.*

*'Sixteenth-century
grating preserved
after the destruction
of Palazzo Morosini del
Giardin at Cannaregio.
It was probably a
balustrade from the
palazzetto'.
Bassi, Palazzi
di Venezia, p. 276.*

Spiriti, and on the right by the palazzo itself. On the side of the Casino, the waters of the northern lagoon provide ever-changing reflections. Towards the lagoon, there is a wall, hidden by a row of trees, serving as a screen against the sometimes-fierce winds. At the end of the garden there is a loggia covered with climbers which hide a smaller secret inner garden. This hidden garden is protected by trees from other houses on the opposite side of the Misericordia and by a gate.

A very well-designed gate in the center of the garden allows entry to the secret place. Large doors, possibly designed by Sanmicheli, in the middle of the palazzo, are the only architectural elements visible, since all the rest is hidden by foliage. The flat rectangular garden is divided into four rectangles, each one containing complex geometrical forms with flowerbeds and decorative elements and is protected by trees from north winds. Four paths which converge in the center lead to figures in animated poses. As so often in these gardens, we can see lemon trees, orange trees, and citron trees in great urns. The garden follows the scheme of Clarici's treatise of 1726. In the Lodovico Ughi's plan of 1729, this garden can be recognized. The Casino degli Spiriti is there, but the loggia, the secret garden, and the trees have gone. This garden and the Casino were already well-known in the sixteenth century, and were where the intellectuals of the time

(the *Spiriti*), such as Aretino, Sansovino, and Titian, would meet. Today, the building is a home for old people, and is cut off from the rest of Venice.

This garden is growing ever wilder, except for certain areas. If a garden is not cared for, Nature takes control, and it begins to resemble the wild spots described by D'Annunzio in 1916: 'Wild richness; heaps of flowers and piles of grass; roses mixed with vegetables; the jagged leaves of the artichoke intertwined with the corinthian leaves of the acanthus; a violet arch of hanging clematis, lighter than a swarm of bees; along the wall the white cabbages grow fat and look as if bedewed by the moon; all the foliage around the blue rose, blocked as if hardened into ice; tall oleanders – not bushes, but trees –, as on the beaches of the Tyrrhenean; stripes of iris, like the top of a farmyard wall in Fiesole; spots of *rosa canina* along the border of a country road in the Lazio Campagna; grapes and their fresh tendrils, bitter to the taste; currants with their small fruit like shining glass; the early figs, light as the veins in their leaves; plum trees with plums still acerbic, one or two already blond with honey; sour cherries and *amarasche*; a small lawn of untended green; rustic ladders resting against the trunks of trees to collect clusters of red cherries that make you think of the ears of children adorned with coral...'
(G. D'ANNUNZIO, *La Leda senza cigno*, p. 148).

The Metamorphosis of the City

IMPLES. Venetian merchants, travelling far and wide, would bring back, among their treasures, not only rare and exotic plants, but also medicinal plants, which, when possible, were placed in an ambience similar to their original setting. Quite a variety of seeds came in this fashion, mixed with spices, and the earth and marble used as ballast in their boats. In the sixteenth century, Venice and Vienna became important commercial centers for exotic plants and flowers. New varieties were bred, never seen before in Europe. The process started by accident, then systematic breeding became a worthwhile enterprise valued by botanists all over Europe. It is difficult to identify with any certainty the botanists who helped to develop this commercial activity, but we know, from a document of the Piovego (the official Venetian body responsible for the lagoon) that Dottore Gualtieri, in 1330, had already obtained an allotment of land at the extreme point of the isle of Sant'Elena to grow medicinal plants (*pro erbis necessaris arti suae*). Roberto De Visiani, in his *Delle benemerenze...*, wrote: 'This concession and the garden thereby created began the tradition of botanical gardens, a debt we owe to Venice...' (R. DE VISIANI, *Delle benemerenze...*, p. 17).

The Venetian botanical gardens were numerous, although we know very little about the early ones. De Visiani tells us that there were a great many such gardens in the Veneto, and in Venice alone, between 1600 and 1800, there were more botanical gardens than in all of the rest of Italy. The Faculty of Medicine of the University of Padua had at its disposal the simples cultivated in the nearby botanical garden (the oldest one still in existence in the world) started by the Venetians Antonio Michiel and Daniele Barbaro in 1545. Antonio Michiel had a garden in San Trovaso, which was well-known for its exotic plants.

In that period there were a variety of fascinating treatises on botanical matters to be found in Venice, from Dioscorides to Theophrastes, the writings of Pliny, and many others, some of which can be found in the Marciana Library in Venice. This great library has the *Codex* of Benedetto Rinio, entitled *Il libro dei Semplici,* of 1415, in which 443 plants are catalogued, in several different languages, with illustrations by Andrea Amadio. The Marciana also contains the five books of Antonio Michiel, with illustrations by Domenico delle Greche (1555-1576) dedicated to the Dogaressa Loredana Mocenigo Marcello, well-versed in botanical matters, who spent much time in her garden on the Giudecca.

Marin Sanudo, in his journal entry of 29 May 1520 states that Andrea Dandolo, Prior of the *Compagnia della Calza degli Immortali*

Terra garden.
'... with her childlike grace, Sirenetta takes my hand, leading me to a rose-bush on a long stem, and says – Look at the rose! – The rose-bush and the girl seem to become one thing. As she holds the stem between two fingers, the little rose seems to have been born in her hand, like the beginning of a spring metamorphosis'.
D'Annunzio,
Notturno*, p. 234.*

*Casa Torres.
In many cases the gardens have kept the original design and even those that are not used so regularly add a welcome note of contrast amid the urban scene.*

88 previous pages
*Seats in the garden of the Cipriani Hotel on the Giudecca.
In this area, in the sixteenth century, were situated the botanical gardens of the Dogaressa Loredana Mocenigo Marcello, to whom Antonio Michiel dedicated his books on botany.*

on the right
*Garden of the Cipriani Hotel.
Venice and Vienna were the principal trading centres for flowers in the fifteenth and sixteenth centuries. The new species came from all over the known world and were distributed throughout Europe. Venice also sent out plants to the East that were scarcely known there.*

organized a dinner party *alla cortesana e danza* in his orchard on the Giudecca, to celebrate the entrance into the Compagnia of Federico Gonzaga, Duke of Mantua. Near Palazzo Dandolo could be found Palazzo Nani, seat of the *Accademia dei Nobili e di Botanica* and the Mocenigo Marcello garden. In the area formerly occupied by these palaces and the church of San Giovanni, we now find the Cipriani Hotel, whose gardens and orchards are probably the same as those mentioned by Sanudo. Today the guest is greeted by a statue of the young Neptune, riding his sea horse, and emerging from a basin of water lilies of various colors. This is approached through a pergola covered with wisteria. In another large protected area, surrounded by cypress, pomegranate, roses, peonies, Japanese maples, lavender, rhododendron, hortensia, and camellia, we find an unusually large and beautiful swimming pool with large urns of marguerites, at each of the four corners.

Past the dining room, through a thick iron gate, one reaches a secluded area, overlooking the lagoon and the island of La Grazia. A heavy wall of shining ivy is punctuated by red Bacara roses, piercing through at unexpected points. At the end, a lawn slopes gently down to the tennis courts, which are hidden by a hedge, and protected by wire netting draped in climbing ivy.

On the right, two stone benches decorated with two sphinxes – often found in Venice –

stand in the shade of tall poplars, giving the illusion of infinite space. If you look closely you discover there are only about twenty trees, not truly a forest, yet they hide the rows of a large, well-kept and unexpected vineyard.

The great fifteenth- and sixteenth-century painters in Venice, such as Bellini, Carpaccio, Cima da Conegliano and Crivelli, often included foliage and botanical subjects in their great works, demonstrating a keen awareness of unusual and exotic plants and flowers found in Venetian gardens. In the *Madonna and Two Saints* by Cima da Conegliano, at the Gallerie dell'Accademia, we can see the *aquilegia* and the orange-tree. In the *Dead Christ surrounded by Angels*, by Cosmé Tura, orchids are carefully depicted. Tintoretto includes the chrysanthemum in his *Martyrdom of St. Sebastian* in the church of the Madonna dell'Orto. Among the varied botanical gardens in Venice there was one which was particularly rich: 'This garden belonged to the celebrated Lorenzo Patarol, the grandfather of Count Francesco. It includes about 600 plants and bushes, most of them exotic and rare, including about 180 varieties of special roses, most of which are not to be found in the gardens of Italy nor even in most others in Europe. There is also a wide collection of exotic and bizarre plants with variegated leaves; many plants from South Africa and Indonesia; and various bulbs from all over. At the end of the garden there is a

Patarol garden at the Madonna dell'Orto in Cannaregio.
Here was one of the most famous botanical gardens of the day. There were 'about a hundred and eighty species of roses many of which were unknown in the gardens of Italy and maybe in many others in Europe'.
Paganuzzi, Iconografia delle trenta parrocchie di Venezia, *pl. XVI.*

90

Palladian loggia, overlooking the north part of the lagoon. In 1815, Emperor Francis II visited this garden with great pleasure' (G.B. PAGANUZZI, *Iconografia...*, plate XVI).

What remains of this garden is a rectangle opening on the lagoon that has lost almost all of its great variety of plants. Passing the gravelled area near the house, we reach the remains of the earlier garden, divided into two parts. Going toward the lagoon, one first passes a space constructed of artificial hills covered with shady trees and grass. On one of these small hills, on the left, beyond a brick arch, there is a protected area where esoteric or meditative encounters are supposed to have taken place. The intention was surely to create a secluded place where one could talk without being overheard. The thick shade of the garden of the Madonna dell'Orto and the twisting path add a touch of mystery. One then unexpectedly emerges into a bright open space: it is the old botanical garden, now filled with vines and vegetables. At the end, the Palladian loggia still exists, with an arch through which the lagoon can be seen.

Another botanical garden in Cannaregio: 'there was in the old times, a large vineyard belonging to the Osservanti [a Franciscan order]. Part was developed as a botanical garden. After the [Napoleonic] suppression of monasteries and convents of 1812, it became a garden for students of a botanical school' (G.B. PAGANUZZI, *Iconografia...*, plate XVIII).

The garden is now completely transformed. The original false hillocks (once used as cold storage places, with the ice and snow of winter placed within) still exist. Tennis courts cover much of the area now, yet there are still beautiful cedars of Lebanon, and pines from the Himalayas.

D'Annunzio describes the wide open spaces of the Giudecca as follows: 'Orchards, orchards! Everywhere orchards! Once, they were the most beautiful in the world, a Paradise on Earth, as they were called by Andrea Calmo, dedicated to poetry, music and love. One sees through a narrow enclosed path with desolate and abandoned orchards on each side. On the top of the walls, in the interstices of the blood-red bricks, there are stalks of wild self-implanted weeds, trembling or rigid like fingers. The tops of the laurels were bronzed by the setting sun... with its long pergolas, its cypresses, its fruit trees, its lavender bushes, its oleanders, its carnations, its roses, its purpura and its yellow crocus – marvelous and sweet, in the varied colors of its dissolution – the orchard looked lost in the remoteness of the lagoon... The sun embraced it all, penetrating every part, so no shade at all could be found. The air was so still that the dry vine-leaves never dropped, even though dead...' (G. D'ANNUNZIO, *Il fuoco*, p. 425).

Venice, surrounded by water and constructed so closely, has its own special set of climatic conditions. Vegetation is found here

*Rocca garden at the
Zattere.
The hedge is more
protective than the wall.
Putti decorate many
gardens on the Grand
Canal and on the
Giudecca as well.*

91

that usually thrives in much warmer or much colder climates. Even the winds influence the setting: the *bora* freezing north-east wind, and the *scirocco* from Africa, as well as the sea, all contribute to the very special climate of Venice. The sea conserves the heat of summer well into autumn, thus retarding the end of the season, just as winter lingers here longer than elsewhere. The minimum air-temperature is found in January; that of the water, in February. As Alessandro Marcello wrote (in *I giardini di Venezia,* p. 576)'Venice lives in a very special set of climatic conditions which resembles the tension between two extremes which change with the vicissitudes of time'. The enclosed spaces, the walls and fences protect the vegetation, creating climatic transformations which makes it possible for the various plants to survive. The overall climate of the city is formed by a 'mosaic of microclimates', which, as we have seen, range from extremes of heat to extremes of cold, in every enclosed space, whatever the size.

Humidity is another element of fundamental importance. Alessandro Marcello and Mario Padovan analyzed five gardens of particular interest: 1. The garden called *'del mercante'*, on Fondamenta Forlani, number 3144 in Castello, exemplifies an old vegetable garden, with an open paved area in front, probably to display merchandise. 2. The garden of the Knights of Malta, at Corte San Giovanni di Malta, number 3253 in Castello, maintains traces of the beds of the ancient *orto dei Semplici*, as well as the more recent beds of ornamental plants. 3. The Gradenigo garden in Santa Croce, Calle Lunga, number 764, where there is a vegetable garden and fruit trees near the house. 4. The garden at Cannaregio, Fondamenta Venier number 342, known as the Venier garden, was specially designed to provide the maximum of shade, thereby separating it from the rest of the world. 5. In the garden dell'Ospedale Umberto I, in Cannaregio, Fondamenta dei Riformati, the plants were arranged to offer relief to the patients. The beneficial effect was achieved by planting trees at the north end to protect the garden and its visitors from the cold wind, while at the south end flowering plants with beautiful scents were placed so that the breezes delight the convalescents with their delectable fragrance.

Even today the Carmelite Friars produce a medication called melisse-water which serves as an antispasmodic and a stimulant; it is produced by creating an infusion of a lemon-scented herb, picked at the moment they come into bloom, and mixing it with cloves, nutmeg, coriander and roots of angelica. In the second half of the last century these friars reconstructed part of the old cloister between their church and the railway station. There is a large orchard with a typical Venetian *cavana* (boat-shed) that opens on the Rio della Crea. A high wall separates the present cloister from the

*Rocca garden at the
Zattere.
The decorations of
the garden repeat the
natural motifs both
in iron and stone.*

*Garden of the former
Palazzo Contarini.
'The following day,
toward sunset, we
visited that northern
garden located between
Madonna dell'Orto and
Sacca della Misericordia,
created by Tomaso
Contarini, Procurator
of San Marco... It is
skilfully composed like
the ground floors of a
palace of greenery'.
D'Annunzio,* La Leda
senza cigno, *p. 150.*

station. This entire area used to be orchards.
The local products were so well-appreciated, in
the old days, that even Aretino's 'greed' was
testimony to their excellence. 'How can one
balance the sour taste of vegetables with the
sweet taste of herbs? It is no mean skill to
mitigate the bitterness of some with the
sharpness of others, so that we can create a
composition, so gentle that the scent of the
mixture is almost enough to satisfy our longing.
The flowers, growing here and there among the
sharp herbs, whet the appetite, making me so
hungry, that I wish to smell them, grab them
into my hands, press them to my nose – almost,
but not quite – a substitute for consuming the
delicious fruit and vegetable on the spot... A
handful of the fruits of these orchards is far
more valuable than the produce of the
best-cultivated gardens elsewhere. I'm amazed
that poets don't fall down on their knees to sing
the praises of the vegetation that grows here.
We do a disservice to the monks and nuns who
create these marvelous greens by not
acknowledging their great contribution to the
pleasures their fruits provide us, since they steal
hours away from their devotions and prayers to
nurse, feed, water and protect the beautiful
vegetation' (P. ARETINO, *Lettere*, libro I, n. 217).

The fresh water to be found in Venice, in the
midst of the lagoon – the vast 'sea' surrounding
Venice – has always astounded visitors. The
sources of fresh water were twofold: wells, dug

deep into the earth, reaching the fresh-water
table to be found below, and great cisterns
designed to collect rainwater. Sansovino
describes the cisterns which collected the
rainwater from the surrounding homes:
'All around the roofs of the homes of Venice
there are gutters of Istrian stone conducting the
water into large cisterns – often public,
sometimes private –. The collected rainwater is
much preferred over well-water for drinking
and for other purposes, since it is sweeter and
softer than the water in wells, which often
contains unpleasant tastes, due to the harshness
of the earth whence the well-water emerges. The
city is well-furnished with these wells and
cisterns, both public and private ones' (F.
SANSOVINO, *Venetia città nobilissima...*, p. 382).

There were once more than 6000 wells in
Venice, both public and private, but they were
closed around 1885, when the acqueduct was
created. In San Barnaba, at number 2885 on
Calle Sporca de le Pazienze, an old brick cistern
covered by a wellhead still exists. It is in the
shade, in the center of a series of small
vegetable gardens, separated by walls. The
rainwater used to be collected from the roofs of
the surrounding buildings, and flowed down in
channels running along the tops of the
separating walls at a very slight incline, and
thereby lost its impurities and was
well-oxygenated, penetrating through grates
into covered pools where the water was filtered

Courtyard of Palazzo Barbaro, the Venetian residence of Henry James, a frequent guest of the Curtis family.

96

previous pages
A very special garden is that of the Orsoni mosaicists, near the Cannaregio Canal. The inner court is indispensable for mixing and blending the colours.

on the right
Courtyard of the Abbazia della Misericordia in Cannaregio.

through pebbles and sand, and then entered the large cistern in the center. During a dry period, in spite of the continuing attempts to collect water at all times, a drought could occur, leaving the cisterns empty.

'Every public Campo (square) and courtyard had cisterns built by the city authorities and funds, at different periods. During the time of Doge Francesco Foscari (1423-1457), when it did not rain from November to February, the Doge ordered that 30 new cisterns be created for the use of the poor, and additional water was also brought from the River Brenta by boat; thus the defects of the season were remedied by skill' (M. SANUDO, *La città di Venezia*, p. 37).

And Sanudo wrote in his journal: 'Venice abounds in everything except fresh-water, for it is in the midst of water but has no water. There are wells and cisterns throughout the city in every quarter, yet, at times of scarcity and drought it is necessary to buy water, brought by special boats, from Liza Fusina, five miles away'.

The fruits of the kitchen gardens follow the mystery of nature, going through the unending cycle of birth, death, and rebirth. D'Annunzio once again caught the rhythms:
'Sirenetta knows all of the secrets of the garden, in all of its complex detail. She knows where the caterpillar hides, where the bee, the spider and the beetle are actively at work. She knows which trees are sick; she knows where buds can be found, when they appear, when they will come into bloom. She complains about the lazy gardener. She takes a bellows to spray the proper powder on the rose bushes covered with squirming green insects. She leads me, with sweet sympathy, to a large white rose, the very heart of which is being devoured by a beetle. – Why don't you just brush away the insect? – I ask – The rose is already lost, and if the beetle is not satiated, it will go and destroy another flower. – I feel that her sympathies are divided between the insect and the flower...' (G. D'ANNUNZIO, *Notturno*, p. 235).

REPOSITORIES. In addition to the gardens, there are open spaces, fenced in and protected. Various craftsmen, such as carpenters, stone cutters, masons, etc., need spaces to keep their stock-in-trade ready for their work. The names of various streets, alleys, and squares remind us of the history of these various storage places. One feels almost obliged to remember the varied activities carried on in the past, which the names of places help us to recall, such as Calle delle Pietre Vive, Barbaria delle Tole.

'These wood-sheds are curious and charming places, with their delicate and pervasive perfume of the pine, the interminable vistas of planks arranged like the letter A, the long grassy walks between each file, and the boundary walls that are mantled deep in ivy' (H.F. BROWN, *Life in the Lagoons*, p. 127). Another example is the Campiello delle Stroppe: 'It was here, perhaps,

*Former Palazzo
Contarini on the
Grand Canal.
Authentic statues
or imitations give
the visitor a sense
of the timeless.*

98

*Decorations in wrought
iron; in the background
the gate of the Palazzo
Brandolini d'Adda,
looking onto the
Grand Canal near
San Barnaba, is
decorated with iron
scorpions, symbols
that are part of the
family's coat-of-arms.*

that the slender willow-branches grew that were used to tie the vines...' (G. TASSINI, *Curiosità veneziane...,* p. 658). *Stroppe* were the elastic young branches of the willow tree.

The names of the streets, alleys and squares help us to remember a time when the streets buzzed with activity and when merchants were busily engaged with bargaining and haggling... 'Merchandise runs through that town like water in a sluice. Venice, built on the sea, with water that runs through and around everything, except the homes and the streets. The citizens can return home by way of the land, or by way of water' (M. DA CANAL, *Les histoires de Venise,* part I, 2-4, p. 5).

In a letter to his landlord, Domenico Bolani, Aretino noted and praised the hustle and bustle of the area of the Rialto, the pivot of the commercial and financial life of the city. 'I would feel remiss if I did not praise the lovely central location of your house where I am living now, providing me with the greatest pleasure of my life, right here in the heart of the Rialto... Whoever built this house chose the best spot on the Grand Canal (the Patriarch of all Canals). Venice, the popess of all the cities in the world, provides me with the happiest, merriest, most joyful life, and the house allows me to look out on the most jocund prospect. I never gaze out of my windows without seeing thousands of people, hundreds if not thousands of gondolas, all active during the times when the merchants

are at their trade. The squares to my right are those of the butchers' and the fishmongers' markets. To my left I see the Rialto bridge and the warehouse of the Germans. In front of me I see the Rialto, filled with people busily engaged in a multitude of activities. In the boats I see grapes, in the shops, game and snared wild birds. There is no need for me to long for irrigated meadows, since at dawn I can marvel at waters covered with an endless flow of merchandise of all seasons. It is great fun to observe the people who bring all this merchandise into Venice as they distribute their ware to their proper places. It is all a joke, except for the score of boats filled with melons. When they arrive together, all at once, with their many-colored sails spread, filled with melons, they look like an island. Then everyone runs to touch, to smell, to weigh, to test the quality of the goods' (P. ARETINO, *Lettere*, libro I, n. 213).

There are still craftsmen who have to use open spaces to practice their profession today. For example, the stone cutters have most of their workshops overlooking the lagoon, so they can receive their heavy wares directly from the boats. Another kind of repository is that of the mosaicists, Orsoni, near the Cannaregio Canal. In addition to being sheltered, the open space is indispensable for mixing and blending the colors. In one part of the garden there are pieces of glass, vats, colored heaps of mosaics.

Bellinato garden in Cannaregio.
'A garden is not made in a year... It is difficult to take leave of one's garden... Though it is not altogether a selfish mistress, it is so all-absorbing'.
Eden, *A Garden in Venice, p. 134.*

102

previous pages
*Brandolini d'Adda garden.
The hedge in the shape of a heart is a rare example of topiary art.*

on the right
The thick shade of the Balboni garden in Dorsoduro.

Behind a grating, there is a more protected area, with a persimmon tree, a palm and a Judas-tree. Roses grow around the iron grating and the wall is festooned with ivy and wisteria. Proceeding towards the furnace, great vats contain the traces of previous mixtures and wooden chests are full of tiles of various sizes and colors, ready for use. Looking from the garden windows one can see a collection of about 7000 different colored tiles from the deposit within where the boards of glass paste are arranged according to their different nuances. The city of rare colors, of shimmering lights and reverberations, here finds a faithful copy of itself.

MEDITATION. 'There are still many other gardens in Venice. I shall never forget the one at the Giudecca, which can be seen from the lagoon, with its copses. I penetrated it once – it is large and silent, and one can walk on and on forever. You breathe the air of the sea. It urges one to think aloud, and sing in a soft voice' (H. DE RÉGNIER, *Esquisses vénitiennes*, p. 11).

The long stretch of land that runs along the left side of Venice has always fascinated visitors. Even today, on the Giudecca, we find the largest gardens, also the most difficult to visit. The houses lining the Giudecca Canal serve as a curtain protecting large green areas from the north wind. But on the lagoon side the island appears as a long strip of green with trees, bushes, vines, orchards, and flowers. Enormous roots of great overhanging trees look as if water-born; they were planted there centuries ago to contain the earth – one of the rarest and most valuable commodities in Venice. The Giudecca still contains closed orders of monks and nuns who have their own orchards and vegetable gardens, tiny oases of green. Here, poets, philosophers, and *letterati*, found a peaceful retreat for their reflections. In his letters Aretino talks of a lady who had withdrawn into a closed order of nuns in this part of the city. He wrote to her, stating that he both despaired at never being able to see her again, and was strangely pleased because: '... imagination does not deprive us of the beauty that once was yours, and therefore will never vanish. I am sorry because I cannot look into the eyes of one who, so valiantly, has shown her contempt for the despised world and has thus overcome fortune. The loss of your husband, your son, your noble status, has given you a recompensation, a reward for your suffering that not even an emperor could grant: the circle within which you enclose your sacred self is greater than all the fields of the moon. Although it may seem small it is a model of that Paradise that you know how to gain, whose walls cannot be conquered by troops or arms... Where you are, Time and Death have no meaning since growing old and dying cannot trouble or hurt you. Blessed are you that know

*The Giudecca still
has the highest number
of vegetable gardens
in Venice. In the
background the
Chiesa della Croce.*

104

how to obtain peace for your body and
salvation for your soul! Let those who are able
to bear suspicion, cares, wars and cruelty rule
over us; and let those who wish to enjoy
security, liberty, peace and piety remove
themselves from us' (P. ARETINO, *Lettere*, libro
I, n. 289).

At the Redentore, beyond the small cloisters
with their ancient olive tree and the refectory,
there is a wide area that lies open toward the
lagoon, protected on the right by a large
building that houses the Seminarians, and, on
the left by a wall that separates the area from
the Sacerdoti garden and Ca' Leon garden.
This area is divided into three zones, cultivated
with edible thistle, artichokes, lettuce, cabbage,
beans, and various fruit trees. There are long
rows of grape vines bordering the paths. There
are several fruit trees and a precious *sorbe* tree.
Along the wall are ranged fig trees offering
shade to fourteen beehives. At the end of the
central section, there is a pigsty with six pigs
and a hayloft and a potting shed for tools and
for the carpenters' workshop. Still further on,
there is the *cavana* (boat-shed) – a prerogative
of monasteries. On each side of the *cavana*,
paths lead to quiet places for meditation, facing
the lagoon. Coolness, privacy and shade
provide wonderful settings for peace, quiet,
reflection, meditation, and prayer.

In the orchard of the Poor Clares, a strict
order of Franciscan nuns, there is a Madonna
crowned by a rose-covered *berceau* near the
house. On each side there are high walls with
vine-covered pergolas, between which we can
still find a large area filled with edible vegetation
of all sorts. Further on, toward the lagoon, there
are also fruit trees of many varieties. Good and
patient care have maintained a piece of real
countryside, here in the midst of the city.

'A garden is not made in a year; indeed it is
never made in the sense of finality. It grows, and
with the labor of love should go on growing.
There are old gardens that one might fear to
touch... It is difficult to take leave of one's
garden, even in writing. Though it is not an
altogether selfish mistress, it is so all-absorbing
that even if one had the pen of a great
word-painter, and could say all one would wish
to say, one might easily dawdle too long over its
lilies and roses, as a young man is prone to do
over his lady's charms and perfections. I will
leave mine, then, advising those who have not a
garden to get one. Those who have, to work in
it. Those who have children, to bring them up
with a taste for it. I was given a garden of my

*Convent of Poor Clares
on the Giudecca.
Convents of enclosed
orders in this area
cultivate small holdings.*

own, a rake and a spade, when I could scarcely walk, and can remember still my delight when I saw the oats I had taken from the stable cornbin begin to sprout. There is no pursuit, as has been found by big men and small, that will so readily and healthily take a man out of himself, and away from his griefs, physical or moral. If the passion for games and athletics may, as we are told, be carried too far, surely that for a garden cannot be. If football and cricket may too soon be too much for us; if bridge all day, as well as all night, is not, or may not be, entirely healthy; gardening must be so always, and will give us occupation and delight from one's earliest days to one's end, making even the weary strive to postpone that end from the longing to see the next year's blossom. God Almighty, Bacon tells us, planted a garden. What can we do better, who can so little do, than humbly yet lovingly strive to make another?' (F. EDEN, *A Garden in Venice*, p. 134).

Francis Eden, who lived on the Giudecca at the turn of the century, wrote in a manner that takes us back to the sensibilities of that time. Behind the convent della Croce, he succeeded in transforming a wild neglected orchard near the lagoon to a carefully planned garden ('The Garden of Eden') well worth visiting. He was looking for a home with a garden, since the city, surrounded by salt water, made him intolerant and 'sick of Venetian stones', of 'pink and gray'. 'I need dry earth, green trees, bushes and

flowers: a garden'. In a plain style he documents the habits of the local people. 'There are three beautiful kinds of pergola that I know... The pergola is sometimes made of iron. The heat of the metal in a hot climate hurts the vine and its material offends the eye... The other forms of pergola that I know, and that are practical and lovely may be seen, amongst many other places, at Amalfi, Gravosa and Venice. I have lately seen a pergola of masonry at Venice in a garden bought by lady Radnor. But there is only one line of columns (the crossbeams resting at the outer wall that protects the garden from the canal outside). The path underneath is paved and sunk some two feet below the surface of the ground and the result is charming... The pergolas in general use at Venice are of other and very evanescent kind. The pollard willows that grow in the low lands of the neighboring *terra-firma* supply the poles... the initial cost is small, and so well suited to Venetian habits; but it is not a cheap vine support, as the soft wood, quickly grown, quickly decays, and requires constant renewal. The upright *pali*, planted about two metres apart in a line on either side of the foot-way, are first connected with *cordoni*, as the laterals are called, at from five to eight feet from the ground, according to the strength of the vines and their owners' requirements for use or appearance. Then the two lines, six to eight feet apart, are joined and made interdependent by

*Gozzi garden on the
Giudecca.
The swimming-pool
dressing-rooms.*

cross poles, *traversi*... On these *traversi* are laid two longitudinal lines constructed of the lighter poles, and the worn *pali* and *cordoni* judged not strong enough for their former service... The whole is bound together by osier bands called *stroppe*...' (F. EDEN, *A Garden in Venice*, p. 33).

Eden is talking of a garden that no longer exists; a garden that cannot be visited is a garden lost forever.

Paolo Bartolomeo Clarici, a botanist at the end of the seventeenth century, in his treatise on the cultivation of gardens, gave suggestions for choosing trees and flowers of appropriate colors and forms. He criticised the gardeners of Venice for their failure to be 'modern' and their rejection of new theories from abroad, specifically those from France and the botanists and gardens of the Sun King. He insists on the need for gardens to be looked after continuously, and provides specific directions on how to choose a gardener. 'The Gardener, if possible, should be of tried faith and well-disposed towards his Master, and not anxious to prove more knowledgeable than him. He should not go walking around the town and visiting hostelries. He should have no pleasures or loves, other than his garden. He should be of robust constitution; not too tall, because he must always bend and kneel. He should know about flowers, and be eager to learn more each day regarding their proper care. He must be diligent in ridding the garden of

harmful insects and animals. He should know the four principal winds, so that he may select the proper site for each plant... He should be aware of the signs predicting weather: the phases of the moon, the action of the sun, the movements of the constellations in the sky which are predictive of the best growth in the garden. He should also be able to draw a plan, and to realize it on earth. Finally he should have all the good qualities that are desired in a master of agriculture. All of the above, a condition to be profoundly desired, but difficult to obtain today' (P.B. CLARICI, *Historia e coltura*..., p. 31).

In an uncontrolled garden, Nature takes over, and defeats human effort. And while untamed nature's only rule is that of self-perpetuation, in an ordered garden nature is planned and projected according to the idea that each person has of the Earthly Paradise. When Nature is thus domesticated it facilitates the processes of meditation and reflection. Regulating nature means gaining control and dominion over what is unforeseeable.

The structure of the Venetian garden aims to enrich and vary the flatness of the terrain. The pergolas provide isolation, company and protection. Gardens too were subject to fashion; those in power had to exhibit their luxury and wealth, and they thus dictated the rules for the lay-out of gardens. In the eighteenth century, the countryside came to be seen as superior in moral and spiritual terms to

*Lazzarini garden in
Dorsoduro.
Today there is a group
of gardens here that are
unimaginable from
outside. They are
nineteenth-century in
origin, created after
various houses were
demolished, and
subdivided after various
changes of ownership.*

107

the city, and thus new ideas arose on how to plan nature. The artisans in charge of such projects saw themselves as modellers, if not sculptors of greenery. Organising and controlling nature became a prime requirement. Even as early as the end of the seventeenth century Clarici, reflecting on the 'marvellous works of God', the creator of all beauty from the heavens to the tiniest 'young shoots', observed 'how Man has reduced by art what is the only office of Nature, and how in many things art has managed to imitate Nature, and the latter has in many other things conferred the benefit of art... on the one hand, art not being the prime operator, it is Nature, assisted and served by Man, that becomes more fruitful and more graceful; but on the other hand I have also observed how art itself sometimes surpasses the works of Nature, and sometimes surpasses those that it itself has created'. The problem of planning a large garden was particularly felt in England, where Lancelot Brown interpreted this new spirit with great skill (which earned him the sobriquet of 'Capability' Brown) by carrying out 'landscape gardening'. This new art-form did not confine itself to laying out paths or trimming hedges, but re-organised whole lakes, rivers, and hills. He substituted himself for Nature itself, operating on a scale that had never been attempted by any gardener before.

What garden is most conducive to meditation? Is it the small enclosed one, with miniature imitations of nature, such as grottoes, small waterfalls and shelters? Or is it the extensive landscape, where the eye ranges over great distances, with natural elements of all colors and varieties? It is very difficult to say. In any event, Venice prescribes limits. The land cannot be extended, and what may seem vast expanses in this city, to a foreign eye can only appear small strips of land stolen from the sea by force. In the old maps we are surprised by the great fragmentation of the gardens, their subdivision into pergolas and protected walks. Mediterranean culture is marked by fragmentation, the tendency to circumscribe and enclose small areas. The clearest example is the labyrinth, in which the area is so compressed as to seem stifling and fatal. The idea of the labyrinth extends from Egyptian tombs, to the Cretan myth of the Minotaur, to Roman gardens, and finally to the Italian and French gardens of the seventeenth century.

This reflects an abhorrence of the *vacuum*, of emptiness. The same tendency can be seen in the detail-crammed patterns of Oriental carpets, such as the one that wrapped Aladdin and bore him down to subterranean caves full of precious stones and jewels, like fruit in summer. And so in Venice, a city where various races and religions have always met, the garden becomes a mystery to decipher, an arabesque to decode, a perpetual journey to the New Jerusalem.

overleaf
*The design of the
pavement can itself
become part of the
decoration. The one on
the right, at the
Guggenheim Collection,
follows eighteenth-
century schemes; the
lozenges have given a
new pattern to the
pavement, which
previously clashed
somewhat with the
sculptures on show. In
the one on the left, in
the cloistered zone of
the convent of the
Redentore on the
Giudecca, the
apparently haphazardly
placed stones add a
touch of mysticism.*

The Hidden Call of the Garden

IMAGINARY. The fantastic is real in Venice. Fantasy provides the strongest sensation of this unique city.

'In the evening, with its bell-shaped chimneys decorated with the changing colors cast by the Sun, vivid pinks, the clearest reds, it seems as if the entire city is a garden, with so many nuances, as if the cultivated gardens in Delft and Haarlem, filled with variegated tulips, has been superimposed upon the city' (M. PROUST, *La fuggitiva*, p. 250).

The pace, tempo and lay-out of Venice are so singular that they oblige the inhabitants to follow a different rhythm from that of any other city. It is a place where the imagination has hegemony over reality. One is seized by an obsession to contemplate and to reflect on appearances. 'The lovely garden of the lagoon... slowly baking in the sun... The roses, the lilies are drooping, the yellowed stems wither... The delphiniums drop their petals, which float down like butterflies losing their wings. The silk of the frail roses is crumpled on their weakened stalks. Thyme, rosemary, all the aromatics seem to burn out like incense. The numerous flowers of the lavender are blue fumes... The pomegranates are aflame, nourished by the red wax of their own balusters. The entire garden wilts and grieves' (G. D'ANNUNZIO, *La Leda senza cigno*, p. 197).

Everything in Venice has its own connotations. The nuances of the sky, the distorted reflections of the stones and ornaments in the water, the flow of the canals – they all leave us with the feeling that this is a city that can only be described, not understood.

'Just as far as the eye could reach, these painted lights were massed together, like a vast garden of many-colored flowers, except that these blossoms were never still; they were ceaselessly gliding in and out, and mingling together, and seducing you into bewildering attempts to follow their mazy evolutions. Here and there a strong red, green, or blue glare from a rocket that was struggling to get away splendidly illuminated all the boats around it. Every gondola that swam by us, with its crescents and pyramids and circles of colored lamps hung aloft, and lighting up the faces of the young and the sweet-scented and lovely below, was a picture; and the reflections of those lights, so long, so slender, so numberless, so many-colored and so distorted and wrinkled by the waves, was a picture likewise, and one that was enchantingly beautiful' (M. TWAIN, *Innocents Abroad*, p. 221). This description of the feast of the Redentore is a pretext to bind writer and reader together in a single emotion, provoked by a common memory.

There can never be enough color, enough light and enough decoration for Venetians. They turn to electric lighting, to fireworks and

113

Chimneys of Ca' Dario. 'And if those natures and architectures / could be summed up in 'me-you' / melted, watered down in lights / with (or) for enigmatic sense / and metaphorical sentiments / And if arms-in-me arm-in-you / could close in the raving gesticulation of a sudden benediction waisting no time / Then patient quotations / would have an explanation: to fall in love'. Cristiana Moldi Ravenna

*Rocca garden
on the Zattere.*

114

on the right
*Palazzo Falier at San
Vitale.*
*'It was in one corner
of an old palazzo
on the Grand Canal,
and the window of the
little parlor looked
down upon the water,
which had made friends
with its painted ceiling,
and bestowed
tremulous, golden
smiles upon it when the
sun shone...' Howells,*
Venetian Life, *p. 88.*

swirling movement in a paradoxical attempt to imitate nature – or at least the emotions that nature arouses. 'A tune accompanied the wave-like dream, one he had already heard in the museum, trickling slowly and sonorously from a small metal music-box, wound by a key, with a glass garden in which lovers adorned with daisies, danced around a fountain of chalcedony' (G. D'ANNUNZIO, *Il fuoco,* p. 400).

The art of miniature gardens in glass and silk began in Venice and later spread throughout Europe. The master craftsmen and glass-blowers had acquired the art of transforming glass into crystal on visits to Bohemia, and they then indulged their whims, inventing new forms for the delectation of the nobles, enlivening their tables at banquets, balls and intimate dinners. Giuseppe Briati was the most famous and the most hated of the great glass-blowers of the eighteenth century. He was so envied by his competitors that he had to leave Murano and establish his home and workshop at the Carmini, where the Fondamenta is still named after him. Cicogna said of him: 'This master had the most brilliant creative ability: there was not one object he could not make in miniature – flowers, fruits, bridges, gardens, animals and figures, all made perfectly. At that time, all the nobles would pompously enrich their tables, covering them with many ornaments, called *dezerts.* Previously, they had been of paste, sugar, porcelain, but all of these

were replaced by Briati glass. Even the Doge embellished his table at public banquets with these marvelous glass objects' (G. TASSINI, *Curiosità veneziane...,* p. 103).

De Régnier too was amazed by the spectacle of miniature gardens: 'Before the one I am about to describe, please remain silent in order to appreciate the surprises to come! Oh, the bizarre garden. Can there be a garden more unusual and more melancholy in its huge littleness? Its elegance is comparable to its complications. There are symmetrical beds, paths to divide it, balustrades to surround it, porticoes to end it, innumerable vases with tiny flowers. It is austere and eternal. This garden is beyond seasons, since it is all in glass, glass of every color, in imitation of a lawn, a column, a rose and a fountain. The eyes feast on the wonders of this amusing and fascinating garden which now amuses the visitors to the Museum and which once, on the table of patricians, attracted the eyes of the noblewomen in Venice with its delicate, fragile and bizarre artifice' (H. DE RÉGNIER, *Esquisses vénitiennes*, p. 12).

Gardens were not only beautifully constructed in glass, but also in gold. 'A great ceremony for the Procurators of San Marco, the Grand Chancellors of the *Scuole,* or the Patriarchs of San Pietro in Castello, would commence with a pompous procession through the Merceria. On these occasions, the merchants would vie with each other, placing fanciful

*San Francesco della
Vigna.
Recent structures
beyond the Renaissance
colonnade add a
contemporary note.*

previous pages
*Mocenigo garden on the
Giudecca.
'Venice lives in a most
singular bio-climatic
condition; fences and
walls protect the
vegetation, creating a
climatic transformation
that is often
indispensable for the
survival of the plants.
The overall climate of
the city is formed
by a mosaic of
microclimates'.*
Marcello, La flora urbica
di Venezia, *p. 132.*

decorations in their windows. A goldsmith
might represent a garden with moving figures,
all in gold, with glittering fountains, falling into
silver basins. The 'water' was formed by fine
golden chains, called *manini*' (C. IVANOVICH,
Minerva al tavolino, p. 125).

'Other caprices made with great skill were
also displayed. For example, needlepoint of
great delicacy wherein a great fountain could
be seen with the finest thread, seemingly
crystal, representing water, and, in perspective,
hills and mountains'. The author writes of the
temporary structures constructed in Piazza San
Marco for special occasions. There were
columns and arches shining with silver and
gold; marble pedestals with urns planted with
cedar and orange trees.

Besides gardens in glass, silk and gold, there
was also one – the so-called Iron Garden –
which was not a garden at all in fact, but a store
of weapons at the Arsenale. There is an
engraving in *Artiglieria Veneta*, by Domenico
Gasperoni, entitled *The Weapon Room and the
Iron Garden at the Arsenal*. Inside the great
courtyard, the ammunition for the cannons is
arranged in huge pyramids. There are at least
sixteen large piles of cannonballs. Suits of
armour are all about. The only imaginary touch
is a huge Baroque *Triumph* in the center.

The creation of fabulous temporary
structures was a skill the Venetians did not only
reserve for such festive occasions as Carnival.

For example, in April 1685 three regiments of
the Duke of Brunswick were engaged as
mercenaries to fight the Turks at Morea, and
before they left the Lido the Duke wished to
demonstrate the prowess of his men. He had a
wooden palace built with a large room and
overhanging balconies for the nobility of
Venice to observe the manoeuvres. The walls
and the vault of the hall were covered with leafy
bowers, hung with fruit and flowers. In each of
the four corners, there were sparkling
fountains, and here and there were statues of
men and women, life-sized, with mirrors
reflecting and multiplying the objects. The
floor was carpeted in green.

One project never realized was Alvise
Cornaro's plan to create a permanent island
between San Giorgio and San Marco.
'This island can be made easily with little
expense, using the rubble left over from
building works, and also the mud dug out from
the canals... There will be a mountain to be
planted with trees, and crossed by lovely paths,
to allow for sweet promenades. At the summit
there will be a loggia to protect one from the
sun, with a lively fountain of fresh water in the
center. From Piazza San Marco, it will be
possible to see the mountain, the theater, the
loggia, and the fountain as well. Between the
piazza and the mountain there will be room for
many large vessels to enter the port. All of this
will be the most beautiful and amazing

*Fresco by Mariano
Fortuny inside
the homonymous
palazzo of the artist.*

119

spectacle that has ever been seen – or that will ever be seen – on earth' (N. MANGINI, *I teatri di Venezia*, p. 28).

Cornaro, coming from the mainland, conceived of a permanent structure, in contrast with the Venetians, more inclined to the ephemeral. The imaginary often interacts with the future in Venice. There are some strange modern structures that add variety to the landscape, such as the huge abandoned gas containers overlooking the cloisters of San Francesco della Vigna; the large artificial oasis at Angelo Raffaele where elderly men play bowls and grow vegetables; and the greenhouses of the Pinzocchere (spinsters) in Cannaregio. It is easy to forget, for a moment, that one is in a place called 'a museum city'.

One of the most enjoyable private properties is the Terra garden: it is not large and is formed with elements of different periods and styles: a polychromatic glass fountain, an Art Nouveau statue of a languid woman – each element by itself is of no special importance, but the overall ambience is enchanting. The large shady trees contribute to the garden as a whole, creating harmony between Nature and decorative elements. Desire for harmony, luxury and languor emanates from Mariano Fortuny's fresco of a garden: a triumph of foliage and fruits, statues in voluptuous or simply languid poses. The colors, ranging from soft to metallic, remind one that natural light is a distant

memory for many twentieth-century painters. 'Electric Moons' illuminate the canvas...

In the black and white illustrations of *Poliphilus*, we can see a wholly intellectual approach to Nature. In Colonna's text, artificial gardens are described: 'When we reached the orange grove, Telemia told me, – Besides all the beautiful things you have seen, Poliphilus, there are four other things of great worth you must see: the glass garden, the labyrinth, the silk garden and the obelisk, symbol of the Trinity. – She then led me to the left side of the Palace, into a spectacular garden, of subtle artifice, wherein every plant was of precious glass. Beautiful beyond imagination, glass leaves were supported by golden trunks and branches; boxwood and cypress alternated; a multitude of flowers of various colors, forms and precious design. The pistils were of gold; the petals were etched with fine patterns. The columns were encircled by morning glories, reaching toward the capitals... Going to the other side of the palace, I saw a garden no less delightful than the one of glass, it was not only difficult to believe but also to describe. This garden had golden trunks; the lawn, the boxwood, the cypress were in silk. In the middle stood a golden gazebo, covered in precious stones. Urns were filled with flowers of marvelous color. The portico was filled with daisies, and the wall was covered with ivy. The urns were embroidered with gold and silver

overleaf
*Boats become bridges,
first of wood, then of
stone. Today in the
Tagliapietra garden,
behind the church of
San Leonardo, in Strada
Nuova, a bridge of
oriental taste still
connects two artificial
hillocks. It is made of
wood, painted green,
and merges into the
all-pervasive ivy. It
serves to protect and
separate a shady,
tree-sheltered place from
the rest of the garden.*

This garden overlooking the Grand Canal near San Stae was created on the remains of Palazzo Contarini.

Palazzo Barbaro on the Grand Canal. The tradition of the house-cum-warehouse with its double doorway giving both onto the land and the water is still found here.

thread, telling stories of Amours' (F. COLONNA, *Hypnerotomachia Poliphili*).

The labyrinth in *Poliphilus* is a very special one. There are in fact few surviving labyrinths in Italy. Two of them are in the Veneto: at Stra, on the estate of the Villa Pisani, and at Valsanzibio, on the estate of Villa Barbarigo. Though we don't know exactly when the labyrinth became popular, we do know from engravings that in the seventeenth century it became an indispensable element in the gardens of princes and noblemen, along with artificial streams, waterfalls, grottoes and rockeries.

A labyrinth can be formed by high hedges, reproducing the maze at Knossus, or with low hedges, used as decorations of flower beds, recreating the arabesques of the Oriental rug. The labyrinth of Poliphilus is unique, since it is a water labyrinth. It reproduces the convolutions of the canals of Venice, which Colonna certainly knew. Telemia, the constant companion of Poliphilus, climbs with him to the top of a tower and from it he sees a garden, in the shape of a circular labyrinth; instead of pathways there are channels of running water. Thus it cannot be perambulated on foot, but must be navigated. The boat symbolizes Life, and all its difficulties. The labyrinth is 'salubrious' and 'pleasant', filled with a variety of sweet fruit and flowers and 'adorned' with springs. Far from frightening, it cheers and heartens the spirit.

There are seven circuits in the labyrinth,

each one controlled by a tower. Access to the labyrinth is through a bridge. The structure of the labyrinth alludes to the Seven Stages of Life. At the first tower, there is a guardian who draws lots to determine where each entrant may go. The Fortune who guides Poliphilus into his first course, directs him into a pleasant navigable channel, between roses, fragrant plants, and fruit trees. At the second tower there are young girls who accompany the navigator, according to the lot assigned to him by the first guardian. At the third tower there are temptresses, and the current becomes more turbulent. At the fourth tower, athletic women, reminiscent of Amazons, control the wanderers, while the current becomes stronger and the rowing more strenuous. At the fifth tower, the water becomes calm and it is now possible to see one's reflection in the water, and a sense of felicity returns. At the sixth tower, 'chaste matrons' are in prayer, while at the final tower the wanderer repudiates his past, and approaches the final circuit. There, the air become dark; the current becomes a whirlpool, and a Greek inscription announces that the navigator is entering the jaws of the wolves of the gods. At the center stands a matron who judges, but, nevertheless, the dragon-like monster is able to move anywhere, ready to devour the wanderer.

The idea that the *Poliphilus* could be set in Venice is a fascinating one. The knowledge

'Next is the comfortable Balbi Valier, with a motor launch called the Rose of Devon moored to its posts, and a pleasant garden where the Palazzo Paradiso once stood'.
Lucas, A Wanderer in Venice, p. 98.

shown of events in this city, the description of certain objects – for example the coral candelabrum, some rare plants – and a certain decorative excess, all suggest that Venice provided a setting – or at least an inspiration – for some of the scenes described by Colonna.

SPECTACULAR. Venice is both the protagonist and observer of events; it is a city of spectacle *par excellence*. The theatrical nature of its geography leads one to expect a new surprise at every turn. Walking the narrow alleys, one is constantly surprised by changing views: squares and Campielli, elegant palaces, humble dwellings, glorious statuary, fountains and gates, so that the marble, brick and porphyry act as antitheses to the water that reflects and multiplies everything. Nature too, which varies with each season, enriches or increases the melancholy of the scene. The green and simple plants that grow in every crack of the stones of Venice underline the unvanquishable persistence of Nature. The shabbiness that is visible everywhere makes it difficult to conceive the former glory of the Serenissima. The past splendour is momentarily revived in a somewhat artificial manner. Venice has now become merely a stage, a place where old dramas are re-enacted. The cast of characters may change, but the mime remains the same. With the revival of Carnival, the *Compagnia delle Calze* (Company of the stockings) has

been brought back to life. These companies date from the fifteenth century. The members wore stockings of bright colors, a different one for each leg. Their other garments were equally splendid. On their thighs they wore the emblem of the different *Compagnie*, elegantly decorated and designed. The *Compagnie*, or Circles, were composed of the sons of nobles, and their function was to organize festivals and other public events. They included the *Sempiterni* (the Everlasting), *Reali* (the Royals), *Fedeli* (the Faithful), *Modesti* (the Modest), *Accesi* (the Flaming Ones), *Ortolani* (the Market Gardeners), and *Zardinieri* (the Gardeners). From 1400 to 1562, there were 43 of these *Compagnie*.

In order to found a *Compagnia*, a license from the Council of Ten was needed. The members composed their own statutes. They distributed the various titles among their members, and officers could hire the services of an architect or poet. The young patricians based their activities on the ancient myths, and took great pleasure in interpreting them poetically. Gatherings and parties of the *Compagnie* were held in public and private places, in patrician homes and often in open spaces. In the city, spectacles were frequently put on, often with striking temporary structures. We have many records of these shows, although few precise ones. Contemporary descriptions are often

*Fullin garden.
Ancient wisteria,
centuries old, can be
found in many gardens.
It is one of the favourite
climbing plants in
Venice: there are
examples in the
Bennati, Levi-Morenos,
and Rocca gardens,
and that of the
Pensione Accademia.*

exaggerated or embroidered, glorifying the marvels of the entertainment, for which no expense was spared with regard to materials and costumes. The *Compagnie delle Calze* organized festivals and spectacles, particularly during Carnival. They used both open and partially enclosed spaces for these occasions, creating temporary structures that were destroyed after use. In 1542, a theater was constructed in a partially enclosed space – the exact location is not known – on the occasion of the performance of *Talanta* by Aretino, commissioned by the *Sempiterni*. The scenery was designed by Vasari, who describes this event: 'In the foreground of the scenery in act I, all done in *chiaroscuro*, there is a Venice represented by Adria, sitting on a rock in the middle of the sea with a coral branch in her hand, surrounded by Neptune, Thetis, Proteus, Nereus, Glaucus, Palaemon, and other sea gods and nymphs, all paying homage to Adria, offering her jewels, pearls, and gold, as well as other riches from the sea. All around were Cupids, throwing their darts of Love, while others hovered in the air, scattering fragrant flowers. All around were beautiful palm trees. In the second act, the rivers Drava and Sava lay nude with their vases. In the third act, we had the river Po, large and corpulent, with seven children representing the seven tributaries of the great Po, as if each one were itself a river of importance, emptying into the sea. In the fourth

act, we find the personification of the Brenta, with other rivers from Friuli. On the other side, facing Adria, is the island of Candia, where we find the god Jove sucking milk from the teat of a she-goat, surrounded by nymphs. Nearby, in front of the river Drava, lies the Tagliamento, and the mountains of the Cadore. Under this, opposite the river Po, are the lakes Benacus and Mincio, which flow into the Po. On the side, and opposite the Brenta, was the river Adige and the Tesino, flowing into the sea' (G. VASARI, *Le vite de' più eccellenti pittori...*, pp. 223-224).

The lighting of the room where the performance was held was particularly remarkable. High up along the walls there was a frieze, 'with a great number of lamps behind balls of glass filled with glistening water which gave great luminosity to the room' (G. VASARI, *Le vite de' più eccellenti pittori...*, pp. 223-224).

Vasari's description still survives; he, on the other hand, saw his own spectacular creation destroyed. This was the custom with the Venetians; once the apparatus for these fine entertainments had been used once, it was never adopted again. We have no idea where the theater was. All we have is a laconic statement by Sansovino, in which he says, 'Last night, a comedy was performed, for which a great many ducats were expended' (F. SANSOVINO, *Venetia città nobilissima...*, p. 152).

The importance of these *Compagnie delle Calze* was supreme. Another company, that of

overleaf
*Adolfo Baldissera
garden.
The fundamental
characteristic of
Venetian life, a
continual interchange
between public and
private, is maintained
in the structure
of the garden as well.*

Rio del Batello. Travelling along the canals, the other road system of Venice, one finds gardens that flank the water but which are no less protected.

The proud battlements of the Mulino Stucky symbolise the importance of industrial civilisation.

the *Accesi* (the Flaming ones) commissioned Palladio to build a theater in Venice. We are certain of the existence of this theater, and the date, 1565, but we don't know where it was situated, because the documents are missing. The plays in Palladio's theater were particularly salacious and scandalized visitors, such as Antonio Persio, from Matera, who wrote in his *Trattato dei portamenti della Signoria di Venetia verso la Santa Chiesa* (1607): 'During the time I stayed there, comedies were presented, in temporary buildings or amphitheaters built at great cost, attended by almost all the nobles, who encouraged the comedians to say the most vulgar things possible. They would take along their wives and daughters. The Jesuits were much opposed to this and they put a stop to it... To prevent this lascivious way of performing comedies they petitioned the Senators, pointing out that in such buildings, so full of people, most of whom were nobles, since it was they who had rented all the boxes, it would be all too easy for someone to use some mechanism to burn and destroy the building and thus to wipe out a great portion of the Venetian nobility. After much discussion in the Senate, the authorities, realising how dangerous this was for the city, prohibited the performance of comedies and ordered the building to be pulled down, to the great loss of those who had built it'.

One theater was certainly in a private garden in Cannaregio, for which we have not only documents but also a precise reference to the place, and even illustrations of the scene, in which the courtyard of the palazzo of Prince Altieri can be recognised. This garden was used at least twice for theatrical performances. The first event for which we have documentation was a performance of *Gl'Amori fortunati negli equivoci* in 1690. The second, in 1697, was on the occasion of the marriage of Duke Emilio Altieri to Princess Costanza Chigi. Two anonymous etchings exist of the 1690 performance, in a book printed for the occasion. In one of the etchings, we can recognize the palazzo, overlooking the garden, filled with the invited guests. The *tympanum* and the loggia are clearly depicted. The loggia has three arches in the center, with wings stretching on both sides of five arches each. The courtyard is paved in stone, and bordered by a low wall and a wrought-iron gate, crowned by a split *tympanum*, with a bust in the center. The guests are looking out, dressed in their elegant gowns and wigs, from all positions on the loggia. The caption under the etching is *Teatro dell'udenza*. The second etching shows the garden, where the performance was held. In the foreground are the musicians, and on either side the spectators, with precious fabrics separating the musicians from the spectators. Two actors are standing in the center with an avenue leading

The theatre of the Altieri garden in Cannaregio. In the seventeenth century there were frequent performances in the open air, with a natural background providing the setting. Gl'Amori fortunati ne gli equivoci was performed in 1690 and a pastoral play in 1697, on the occasion of the marriage of Duke Altieri.

back to an arch. On the sides there are numerous trees, also in vanishing perspective, and at the ends of the rows of trees stand four cypresses. On the left, among six urns with lemon trees, three jets of water spout from hillocks of porous stone. Everything corresponds to Martinoni's descriptions, which might otherwise seem exaggerated.

This is one of the few examples of an actual court theater in Venice. In fact, Gasparo Altieri was a Roman and had brought this custom with him. Between 1789 and 1805, the palazzo was demolished. In this theatrical city, the interiors of the palazzi themselves were furnished in specacular fashion, to complement their elaborate exteriors. The salons were furnished sumptuously and even the entrance-hall, with decorated benches and statues, had mirrors that reflected the water outside, creating an effect of overall shimmering. The gardens too, on many occasions, would become a perfect setting for parties and amorous dalliance and banquets. 'I descended into the garden. The guests were scattered along the paths, and under the pergolas. The night air was humid and tepid, so that the delicate eyelids felt the humidity like a gently caressing mouth. The stars hidden by the jasmine gave off a delicate fragrance in the shade; the fruit had the heavier smell of the island-orchards. A vivid force of fertility emanated from that tiny space of fecund earth,

which seemed to be imprisoned in its confining belt of water' (G. D'ANNUNZIO, *Il fuoco*, p. 186).

If a garden is large enough and well-ordered in the arrangement of its spaces, it can easily serve as a true theater for the presentation of performances. Goldoni says in his *Memorie*: 'Venetian comedy can really become theater after the performance. First let me tell you about *i morbinosi*: in the Venetian language, *morbin* means good cheer, entertainment, so that the *morbinosi* can be called persons of good humor and partisans of good cheer. The heart of the comedy we had just seen was historical. One of the lively actors, (a true *morbinoso*) proposed supper in a garden on the island of Giudecca, near Venice. We were a large group of 120 *copains*, seated at one large table, well-served with admirable order and precision. There were no women during supper, but many joined us for fruit and coffee, which gave us the chance to begin a delightful dance, and thus we spent a most pleasurable night. The subject of our comedy was truly a *festa*! Consequently, it required embellishment, with anecdotes, jokes, and comic characters. I found, among our happy company, quite a sufficient number of comedians, and I was able to produce enough jocund effects, without offending anybody!' (C. GOLDONI, *Memorie*, p. 240).

A *festa* in a garden is an occasion for presenting oneself in a different way – to be

*Mocenigo Casagrande
garden in Dorsoduro.
Apart from the bust
in the ivy, and
various ornamental
objects, there are
also contemporary
sculptures.*

131

both actor and audience at the same time.
'The elegant company entertained themselves
in enjoyable pastimes, such as that of the
gardeners, in which men and women, dressed as
gardeners, talked of flowers, using them as
allegories to express sentiment, one of the
forms of symbolic language that delighted both
knights and dames, in which even the colors of
their costumes had conventional amorous
meanings' (P. MOLMENTI, *La storia di Venezia...,*
vol. II, p. 380).

'She wore a striped dress, white and green,
which seemed to be made in the image of one of
those silver poplars, whose branches tremble
delicately in the breeze' (G. D'ANNUNZIO,
Notturno, p. 235).

According to Nicolò Franco, in *La Philena,*
'White signified faith in the beloved person;
rust, firmness and perseverance; green, hope;
yellow, desperation; pink, pain; blue, jealousy;
orange, contentedness; vermilion, revenge and
anger; purple, supreme happiness; ash-grey,
suffering of the soul; *lonato,* strength; violet,
love...'

'The little rose is grafted on to her; it is the
flower of her tenderness. She is so pure, so
fragile, so delicately built that one cannot
compare her to anything corporeal, but only a
chaste ineffable thought... Her perfection is
fleeting. I can almost see her petals opening
from moment to moment. On the first night she
will be completely open and empty...'

(G. D'ANNUNZIO, *Notturno,* p. 235).

People seek one another, moving around the
garden as if they had stepped from a tapestry.
'In the corners of the walls, statues emerge. In
her arms, a woman is holding a model of a
crenellated tower. Lavender-bushes. Poppies.
Imperial poppies. Before entering the garden,
there is an atrium, from which one enters the
main garden through a wrought-iron gate, on
either side of which stand two statues on
pedestals. The statues are of vigorous men,
holding young women in their strong arms,
reminiscent of the Rape of the Sabines. Here
and there, in niches, there are more statues, and
there is a pergola covering the cobble-stoned
path...' (G. D'ANNUNZIO, *Taccuini,* p. 118).

Open-air *feste,* from the sixteenth and
seventeenth centuries to the fall of the
Republic, were among the many licentious
entertainments that the city offered. In the
eighteenth century, Giacomo Casanova
described a water festival in honor of the arrival
of Joseph II, '... an ingenious means was
conceived in order to make the surfaces of the
canals seem like ornate gardens, decorated with
plants and flowers arranged in beautiful
designs' (G. CASANOVA, *Istorie delle turbolenze,*
vol. II, p. 61).

Tassini describes festivals that became
celebrated: 'The eighth of August, 1742, the
day of San Gaetano, the Ducal family of
Modena, accompanied by many gentle

*overleaf
Ca' Zenobio.
In the sixteenth century,
with the diffusion of
humanist ideals, the
idea of the garden as a
perfect place became
widely accepted.*

*Floral decorations in
wrought iron and
concrete imitate nature,
almost as if to arrest its
course and demonstrate
that man can do
what nature cannot.*

Venetian dames, went to the palace of N.V.
Condulmer, in front of the Church of the
Tolentini, to enjoy a party... Lovely
refreshments were served. There was lighting in
the garden, and a noble serenade, all at the
expense of N.V. Condulmer, who was a famous
gambler, and had won a great deal of money
from the hereditary princess...' (G. TASSINI,
Curiosità veneziane..., p. 322).

In these gardens, the spectacle was not only
provided by statues and vases but by rose
bushes, by the *berceau*, present in all gardens
from the noblest to the simplest, by palm-trees,
fig-trees, pomegranates, and exotic plants, all
with their own particular meanings. They were
probably hangovers from ancient pagan rites,
symbols of fertility or protection against illness
and other disasters, and were placed in
appropriate spots in the garden.

The garden, in many cases were both grand
in style, and vast in extent.
'Palazzo Gradenigo, at San Simeon Grande, of
the school of Massari, had such an extensive
garden that one could ride around in it a
four-horse carriage, as was actually the practice
until the end of the last century. In this garden,
they held a bull-fight as well on February 10th
1767' (G. TASSINI, *Curiosità veneziane...,* p. 325).

This garden was destroyed between 1921
and 1922, to create a more rapid transport
route between San Simeon Piccolo and Frari.
The gardens of Palazzo Cappello and Palazzo

*Palazzo Cappello
on Rio Marin.*

Gradenigo were amply described in the last
century. D'Annunzio notes, in his *Taccuini*, the
vegetation of the garden of Palazzo Cappello,
and particularly the dividing line with Palazzo
Gradenigo.
'Palazzo Cappello. The garden. Along the wall
which divided it from the Gradenigo garden, a
line of lilies. Against the wall, vines mixed with
jasmine. The pergolas run along the avenues.
Fruits and flowers; pear-trees, peach, almond,
plum, cherry, medlar, apricot, strawberry...
Whole beds of strawberries. Numerous roses –
carnations gushing from a holy-water stoup.
Rose bushes are trained into curved arches...
Whole beds of red poppies; trees full of
vermilion cherries. Along the damp wall, white
and violet irises' (G. D'ANNUNZIO, *Taccuini*, p.
117).

The names of fruits and flowers here stand
for colors. One can almost smell the perfume
and feel the freshness of the place.

In addition to performances, hunts, water
sports, wooden structures and horse-riding,
Pietro Gradenigo Dolfin in his manuscript tells
of a garden with a chessboard. 'A marble
chessboard of bi-colored square stones forms
part of the pavement of the garden, where two
companies of noblemen and skilled players act
out the game, splendidly arrayed in different
costumes, representing kings, queens, knights,
bishops, castles and pawns' (P. GRADENIGO,
Commemoriali, vol. 8, c. 3).

*'All the nobles would
pompously enrich their
tables, covering them
with many ornaments,
called* dezerts.
*Previously, they had
been made of paste,
sugar, porcelain, but
when Briati
demonstrated his great
inventive skills, all of
these were replaced by
Briati glass. Even the
Doge embellished his
table at public banquets
with these marvelous
glass objects'.*
Tassini, Curiosità
veneziane..., p. 103.

ARCANE. 'The nymph in the center holds an unusual branch of bright red coral, a foot high, placed on an emerald mound, which closes the mouth of an antique vase of gold, similar to a chalice. The golden vase is as high as the mound and the coral together. The vase is finely worked with an ancient technique: the top of the vase is decorated with jewels in the form of an acorn. The rest of the vase is encrusted with jewels. On the branches of the coral, there are flowers, open like a five-petalled rose, some of sapphire and of rubies. In five of these flowers, there are large *pomoli* (knobs), the color of red fruit, strung on golden quills, which emerge from the center of the flower. *Monstrous* pearls decorate the flowerless branches... One of the nymphs offers fruit, plucked from the coral – they have an exquisite taste, never before experienced...' (F. COLONNA, *Hypnerotomachia Poliphili*).

In the Treasury of the Scuola di San Rocco, there still exists a candelabrum described by the scholar Jasminka Pomorišac De Luigi: 'A large branch of light red coral, mounted on a shrine on a large base, which ends in six wide points and six narrow points, has been transformed into an elegant tree of Gothic lines. At different distances from the ends of the two branches two small bowls covered with thorny leaves act as candle-holders. Buds, worked in the same manner, hang from the same branches, and enclose colored pearls. The finest branches have been executed in paste, painted with red, and attached to the coral by small cylinders of gilded metal. In order to heighten the effect of the red of the branches, perhaps, the vertical bands of the architectonic node are painted in opaque black' (*Venezia e la peste,* p. 330).

This object is remarkably similar to the one described in the *Poliphilus*. One imagines that such detailed descriptions must have been inspired by real models, even if further elaborated by the writer's imagination.

Unusual objects can still be found today in this city, where the accumulation of ephemera has long been a custom. Rarities, such as those just described, are conserved and admired by specialists, as well as by amateurs. In the special world of the small Venetian garden, amphorae, inscribed stones, marble remains of statuary capture the attention of anyone who stops to look at them. They are reminders of silent cultures, now lost, often with allusions to unknown heroes, myths and rites.

'At the tip of the Sacca della Misericordia stands the old Casino degli Spiriti, so-called because of the arcane noises widely reported to be audible here, resulting from the winds or echoes, which send back from the Casino all the voices emanating from the extremity of the Fondamenta Nuove – a phenomenon which is considered to be a diabolical presage in popular superstition' (G. TASSINI, *Curiosità veneziane...,* p. 586).

*'On these occasions,
the merchants would
vie with each other,
placing fanciful
decorations in their
windows.
A goldsmith might
represent a garden
with moving figures, all
in gold, with glittering
fountains, falling into
silver basins.
The water was formed
by fine golden chains,
called* manini*'.*
Ivanovich, Minerva al
tavolino, *p. 125.*

'Arcane' here alludes to various exotic or magical practices. The atmosphere of such experiences still lingers in the gardens of Venice. The geometrical lay-out of many gardens suggests an age-long search for cosmic harmony.

'It's the garden of Venice I would love most of all, if I didn't love that of Palazzo Dario, which is perfectly square, divided by regular paths into proper forms. Women dressed in tunics hold up a pergola; they are fat and joyous, with great breasts, ample bellies, with navels well-delineated in the wood in which they are sculpted. They proudly hold up trunks, leaves, vine-leaves, and bunches of grapes. In the background, a fountain splashes into a marble basin, and the sound attempts to supplant the silence drop by drop' (H. DE RÉGNIER, *Esquisses vénitiennes*, p. 10).

That marble basin in which the fountain plays, multiplied by the mirror at the end, renders the small garden of Ca' Dario more hermetic, and, at the same time, more precious. It is not that one manages to find a meaning for each symbol; sometimes, even the absence of explanation makes each detail more enigmatic and somehow significant.

'The image of a staircase signified to him his own ascending; he had already seen it in the abandoned garden, contained within the arms of the loggia of Palazzo Gradenigo...' (G. D'ANNUNZIO, *Il fuoco*, p. 204).

'At the end of the garden there is a small open temple with eight stone columns. On the *tympanum*, there are five statues of the seasons and the naked sun god. On the right, beyond the wall, we can see cypresses, and a great singing pine tree, and the greenish cupola of San Simeon Piccolo. The interior of the temple has faded frescoes on the back wall. A central figure of a woman still conserves the freshness of her skin; and in front of her there is a sort of marble altar on which it is sweet to place flowers' (G. D'ANNUNZIO, *Taccuini*, p. 117).

The remains of emblematic constructions, such as the miniature temple of Palazzo Cappello, testify to the existence of ceremonies of classical memory – even the simple pleasures of strolling and meditating. Pagan divinities, more than any other, have taken over what remains of the garden. There are two statues of the Caesars against the right-hand wall of the paved garden, near the palazzo. This famous garden, utterly abandoned today, retains its fascination in spite of the decay into which it has fallen. Leaving the wide hallway of Palazzo Cappello, the stones in the pavement are in considerable disarray. The wall, separating the paved area from the rest of the garden, is covered with wild vegetation. On the pillars between the two gardens there are still three pairs of statues. In the greenery, overturned and broken statues, covered with moss, testify to past splendor. A hedge of *pitosforo* has invaded the cobble-stoned path. At the end, we can see

137

Engraving taken from Poliphilus. *It bears a curious resemblance to the fourteenth-century candelabrum (46.5 × 36.2 cms) in embossed and gilded silver in the treasury of the Scuola Grande di San Rocco.*

138

on the right
Vegetable gardens on the Giudecca. Overhanging greenery often reveals the presence of a garden to passers-by in the street or the canal. However, such gardens are only a tiny percentage of the total number.

overleaf
'Where are the most beautiful roses? Without doubt in Venice... along the dead lagoon, on the other side of the Giudecca'. Vaudoyer, Les délices de l'Italie*, p. 128. Titian had a beautiful garden with flowers and trees which he entered via an external staircase. It was there that he is said to have studied the famous tree for the painting,* St. Peter the Martyr.

the battered remains of the temple mentioned by D'Annunzio.

Another place charged with mystery and arcane fascination is the Mocenigo Garden at San Sebastiano, to which the pages of Henry de Régnier probably refer: 'I remember one of those gardens, whose name I no longer recall, in the area of San Sebastiano, inhabited by decrepit old statues, once heroes and gods'. (H. DE RÉGNIER, *Esquisses vénitiennes*, p. 10).

The space is very shady; in the middle is a fountain with a basin decorated with statues. On the right is a gazebo with benches, in braided wrought-iron; at the far end an *exedra* with wide arches creates a magic space, where initiation into mystical rites could be held. Modern statues by Hennessy help to emphasize the quality of mystery. The flowers and the fruits also have possible connections with the ancient rites. 'The pomegranates, like chandeliers alight with small flames that are almost flower and almost fruit, almost light and almost wax. The heads of the poppies, tall as the young Proserpina, are crowned with nine points, exuding drowsiness. The tiny carnations in tight bunches which the Venetians call *The Eyes of Christ* and you call *Poet's carnations*, are reminiscent of embroidery on a green silk coat. A carpet of yellow, white and violet pansies; tiny clusters of roses and grapes cascade; ever-blooming roses in bushes, massed in fields...' (G. D'ANNUNZIO,

La Leda senza cigno, p. 148).

Fables are born and evolve to interpret the ineluctable mystery of Nature, sometimes benevolent, sometimes cruel:
'The following day, toward sunset, we visited that northern garden located between the Madonna dell'Orto and Sacca della Misericordia, created by Tomaso Contarini, Procurator of San Marco, brother of Cardinal Gaspare, who was a candid friend of Vittoria Colonna... It is not as wild or as rich as the garden of the Giudecca, a blazing mixture of scents and flavours. Composed with great art on the remains of the sixteenth-century garden, subtly planned, similar to the ground-floor rooms and chambers of a palace of greenery where you live for a Spring like a well-bred lady, though one who is not averse to sully her mild grace with some act of negligence... Nontivolio, with the high steps of a whippet, walked along a floor of white and red squares bordered by boxwood no more ponderous than a garland. Under her high heels, the Verona marble shone like sumptuous porphyry. We went from one apartment to another through corridors consisting of arbors. The pergolas were supported by old columns, old capitals, old beams, and the fronds seemed to lament the loss of their flowers... We entered the music room. The tapestries were green, green the carpets...' (G. D'ANNUNZIO, *La Leda senza cigno*, p. 150).

The Presence of the Absent

INITIATION. Beyond the thick scrub and the artificial hill there lies a pathway. Loose stones, haphazardly arranged, form a low wall that separates the area of green from that set aside for recreational activities at the Patriarchal Seminary. At the end of the wall, providing a lovely finial, there is an ancient marble scroll, carved in the Renaissance manner. The eye follows the concentric evolutions of the scroll; it is an object placed there by chance, which has lost its original function; it was probably an ornament from a staircase. This merely adds to its fascination.

The idea of the arabesque, the volute, the scroll, is at the basis of the design of the maze in the garden of Palazzo Brandolini d'Adda. From the *piano nobile* of the palazzo, one can observe that the low hedge of boxwood takes over the whole area. It becomes a path of initiation, inviting you to follow the narrow passage through the hedges with your own feet, as well as feasting on it with the eye. The maze is an Allegory for Passion or Love: if one is too close to it, the object of Desire is rendered blind. From nearby it merely appears to be a box-wood hedge arranged in narrow pathways; only from a distance does its shape reveal itself. Such open references to amatorial rites are rare in Venice.

Convoluted forms, such as scrolls, characteristic of Renaissance inspiration, can be found in a variety of objects. For example, in a pathway of randomly placed roughly-hewn stones, the single beautifully engraved tile marks the passage from the horizontal lawn to the vertical hedge.

There are many enigmatic details in the open spaces of the gardens, designed under the Neo-Platonic influence of the Renaissance. Allusive details, magic rituals, particularly designed to capture the visitor's attention and to stick in his mind, are found in designated parts of the garden, particularly in the points of passage from one part to another. In the Venetian version of the Renaissance garden it is essential to realize that nothing was left to chance. All elements were carefully planned, including all manner of vegetation. What we see today is the result of centuries of reconstruction, one period following another with its varied tastes. In order to reconstruct the original plan, it is necessary to enter into the mode of thinking and the sensibilities of another age, when the pace of life was slower.

'But we continued in the enjoyment of the beautiful garden... on which our chamber windows looked. It was full of oleanders and roses, and other bright and odorous blooms, which we could enjoy perfectly without knowing their names; and I could hardly say

145

Library of Ca' Zenobio. Figurative details alluding to magical rituals are mostly concentrated in particular spots in the garden: the crossing-points between one part and another.

In the Poliphilus
*there is a detailed
description of the
flowerbed in the garden
of Cythera, the pattern
of which resembles
that on the tile on the
border of the garden of
Palazzo Minotto,
whose Renaissance
proportions contain a
hint of something
more disturbing.*

whether the garden was more charming when it
was in its summer glory, or when, on some rare
winter day, a breath from the mountains had
clothed its tender boughs and sprays with a
light and evanescent flowering of snow.
At any season the lofty palace walls rose over it,
and shut it in a pensive seclusion which was
loved by the old mother of the painter and by
his elderly maiden sister. These often walked on
its moss-grown paths, silent as the roses and
oleanders to which one could have fancied the
blossom of their youth had flown; and
sometimes there came to them there, grave,
black-gowned priests – for the painter's was a
devout family – and talked with them in tones
almost as tranquil as the silence was, save
when one of the ecclesiastics placidly took
snuff... and thereafter, upon a prolonged
search for his handkerchief, blew a
resounding nose. So far as we knew, the garden
walls circumscribed the whole life of these
ladies...' (W. D. HOWELLS, *Venetian Life,*
p. 360).

In Venice, the dimension of time is unique.
What in other cities is an inexplicable obstacle
to work and productivity, here becomes an
advantage. One has to accommodate oneself to
the rhythms and pace of this city if one wishes
to enjoy what it has to offer.

The actual entrance to the garden, or to
some specific part of it, tends to underline the
passage from one place to another, from one

boundary to another, from one bank to another.
Boats became bridges: first in wood, later in
stone.

In the Tagliapietra garden, behind the
church of San Leonardo in Strada Nuova,
there still exists a rare example of a bridge
within the garden itself. Oriental in taste, it
connects two artificial hillocks. It is made of
wood, painted green, and thus merges into the
background of all-pervasive ivy. It is there to
protect and to separate a cool space shaded by
trees and other greenery from the rest of the
garden.

Nature is always present not only in physical
terms, but also with all its subtle and recondite
symbolic meanings. As we enter the garden of
Brandolini d'Adda, ivy frames the huge
entrance door leading the visitor between two
oleanders which prepare one for the change
from the surrounding environment. Two
guardian angels, shaded by the oleanders, add
ambiguity and mystery. Each of these elements
has profound ancient meanings: ivy, as Pliny
pointed out, represented both Death and
Eternal Life: death, because it strangles the
vegetation around which it grows; eternal life,
because it is forever green and difficult to
extirpate.

The oleander, likewise, symbolizes both Life
and Death, since some believe that it saves the
lives of those who sleep in its shade, while
others hold that its poison can cause their

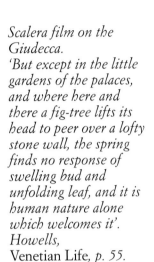

*Scalera film on the
Giudecca.
'But except in the little
gardens of the palaces,
and where here and
there a fig-tree lifts its
head to peer over a lofty
stone wall, the spring
finds no response of
swelling bud and
unfolding leaf, and it is
human nature alone
which welcomes it'.
Howells,*
Venetian Life, *p. 55.*

death. The door thus marks not only a physical but also a symbolic passage. One steps over the threshold, in a metaphorical sense, from one world to another.

Nature acts as a bridge between humanity and divinity – 'our Lord went to the Mount of Olives' (LUKE 22: 39). It is believed by theologians that the Holy Cross was constructed of four different woods: olive, cedar, palm, and cypress, almost as if to prove that the union of all of nature favours the passage from life to death.

Every religious rite has its own form, its own formulae: gestures, words, psalms. Natural elements, such as water, plants, trees and flowers, lead from the mundane toward the supernatural world. Purificatory rites are often necessary at the entrance to sacred places.

We can observe this in Venice, where a font containing holy water stands in the orchard of the Franciscans at the Redentore.

In contrast to the guardian angels at the entrance to the Brandolini d'Adda garden, in Greek mythology we find monsters such as Hydra, and the Cretan Minotaur, allowing entry only to heroes, while ordinary mortals are excluded – or destroyed. Once again, Venice has elements of all the ancient rites and religions of the world: we find monsters supporting stone benches in the garden of the Guggenheim Collection, protecting the ashes of Peggy Guggenheim – and her dogs.

'– Never again? – She walked under the pergolas, toward the water. She stopped on the grassy bank, weary, and sat on a stone. Lowering her head, she put her hands to her temples, making an effort to collect her wits, to regain self-control, to reflect, to deliberate...' (G. D'ANNUNZIO, *Il fuoco,* p. 356).

The theme is that of new worlds: new worlds to discover, worlds of thought, of love and death, worlds to which only the initiates can gain entry.

In medieval literature, in which the pleasures of the *rosa fresca aulentissima* are softened into delicate amorous metaphors, gardens are the stage for daring enterprises. In such works we find rose gardens, fountains, springs, scents and all those symbols which in the east belong to erotic literature. In the Venetian garden luxury and exoticism kept alive the memory of travels to distant lands where nature and the tales it inspired were so different.

'The Venetians delighted in gates wrought in bizarre forms, in vases, arches, balausters, loggias, statues, they revelled in limpid waters, held placidly in marble basins, or flowing through murmuring streams, gushing in cascades through mossy rocks, spouting forth in fine rain, in veils, in gushes and jets of strange shapes; at the front they opened out into symmetrical flowerbeds, elsewhere they closed into dark and shady avenues: these gardens

*Di Thiene garden.
In Venice the temporal
dimension is unique.
One has to respect its
slow rhythms if one
wishes to enjoy what
the city has to offer.*

openly revealed the art that had created them, at least they did not betray a wretched attempt to compete with nature by mimicking her inimitable works...' (R. DE VISIANI, *Delle benemerenze...,* p. 17).

The symbolic garden is always organised along similar lines:
'A garden enclosed is my sister, my spouse, a spring shut up, a fountain sealed.
Thy plants are an orchard of pomegranates, with pleasant fruits, camphire, with spikenard, Spikenard and saffron; calamus and cinnamon, with all trees of frankincense; myrrh and aloes, with all the chief spices:
A fountain of gardens, a well of living water, and streams from Lebanon.
Awake, O north wind; and come, thou south; blow upon my garden, that the spices therefore may flow out. Let my beloved come into his garden, and eat his pleasant fruits.
My beloved is gone down into his garden, to the beds of spices, to feed in the gardens, and to gather lilies.
I am my beloved's, and my beloved is mine: he feedeth among the lilies'
(*The Song of Solomon*: 4, 12-16).

In many engravings and drawings of the medieval world, wooden trellises, small walls, and fences are evident, dividing up the different functions of the garden, so that the agricultural section is divided from the private garden.

The garden of Palazzo Zenobio, today the Armenian College, gives much of this feeling. From the entrance hall, we pass into a courtyard; grillwork, with a gate at the center, then divides the courtyard from the vast open space of the garden, where there are flowerbeds and topiary. At the bottom of the garden stands the library built by Temanza, which recalls the structure of the nymphaeum, the characteristic feature of the most important Venetian gardens. When the visitor reaches the Nymphaeum-Library and looks to his right, the perspective changes, offering unexpected views that suggest different interpretations. It is as if, by leaving the building, the Initiate has taken the first step along a path that will gradually lead him towards the truth. The sinuous lines of two routes indicate two opposite goals. At the centre a wide path splits in two, showing two possibilities. Lingering before a door that opens is a recurring symbol of uncertainty at important stages of life.

In the *Poliphilus* the Threshold becomes an obsession. The door is a symbol of the mode of life that must be chosen. After much hesitation, attempting to choose between the three possibilities – the Door of Heaven, the Door of the World, and the Door of the Pleasure of Love – Poliphilus chooses the Door of Venus. His hesitation reveals itself through the minute description of architectural and natural details,

*overleaf
Marble objects have
often been preserved
because of their beauty
but are sometimes
found fulfilling
functions that are quite
different from that for
which they were
originally created.*

149

Pellegrini garden.
A quiet corner protected
by vines and gateways;
one reaches it by alleys
and lanes that are
virtually secret passages.

on the right
Water-entrance to the
vegetable-garden of the
barefoot Carmelite
friars in Cannaregio.

overleaf
'The rose was also the
flower of pride and of
triumphant love because
it was the flower of
Venus, goddess of
love...' Levi d'Ancona,
The Garden of the
Renaissance, *p. 330.*

but in the end it is curiosity that wins:
'And so I thought: perhaps within there is the
venerable altar of the mysterious sacrifices and
sacred flames, or rather, the statue of the divine
Venus and also of Eros, her dispatcher of the
arrows of love. With great veneration, I put my
foot on the sacred threshold, and suddenly I
saw a white mouse which was running away.
Immediately, without a furthur thought I
entered, my eyes wide-open, and in this shining
place I saw amazing things, out of this world...'
(F. COLONNA, *Hypnerotomachia Poliphili*).

At the end of the last century, closer to our
own time, Aubrey Beardsley in *Under the Hill*
reproposed the theme of Poliphilus in his
version of the legendary trip of Tannhäuser to
Venus, with considerable irony. At the
beginning of the novel, the protagonist finds
himself in a wild wood, at the entrance to the
hill of Venus. It is sunset, 'a delicious moment
to slip into exile'. The protagonist is caught
between two worlds; Nature itself turns
fantastic and wild:
'... huge moths so richly winged they must have
banqueted upon tapestries and royal stuffs,
slept on the pillars that flanked either side of
the gateway, and the eyes of all the moths
remained open, and were burning and bursting
with a mesh of veins' (A. BEARDSLEY, *Under the
Hill: The Story of Venus and Tannhäuser*, p. 25).

The uncultivated garden is often full of
mystery, an inextricable tangle. It may look
merely untidy, but it hides secrets even more
difficult to decode. Like Poliphilus, the abbot
Tannhäuser hesitates, frightened to enter.
Sacred and profane rites, both mediaeval and
Renaissance, intertwine in the moment of
decision:
'A wild rose had caught upon the trimmings of
his muff, and in the first flush of displeasure he
would have struck it brusquely away, and most
severely punished the offending flower. But the
ruffled mood lasted only a moment, for there
was something so deliciously incongruous in
the hardy petal's invasion of so delicate a thing
that Tannhäuser withheld the finger of
resentment, and vowed that the wild rose
should stay where it had clung – a passport, as it
were, from the upper to the underworld' (A.
BEARDSLEY, *Under the Hill: The Story of Venus
and Tannhäuser*, p. 26).

The secret gardens of Venice, which have
inspired so many great thinkers, poets,
architects, continue to have a profound
resonance... For those fortunate enough to
have experienced the relatively few which still
exist, and for the Memory of those which have
disappeared into 'the jaws of the Monsters of
the Gods' – and the ravages of Time, their past
or present existence continues to inspire... And
for those who never before have had any access
to them, may the photographs, quotations and
texts herein contained lead to inspiration and
the mystery of a new vision of ancient Venice.

The authors wish to thank the following authorities:

Mons. Renato Volo, Patriarchal Chancellor

Mons. Giuliano Bertoli, Rector of the Patriarchal Seminary

Padre Raffaele Andonian, Director-General of the Collegio Armeno

Don Ettore Corso, Director of the Congregation of the Sons of Don Orione

Padre Gabriele de Zan, Guardian of the Minor Brothers of San Francesco della Vigna

Padre Cesare Zandonà, Guardian of the Convent of SS. Redentore

Padre Sergio Treccani, Prior of the Barefoot Carmelites

Madre Cesarina, Mother Superior of the Sisters of the Reparation Institute Canal Marovich

Suor Chiara, Superior of the Sisters of Maria Bambina of St. Mary del Soccorso

Suor Giovanna, Mother Abbott of the Monastery Clarisse of the Holy Trinity

Suor Ilia, Superior of the Casa Cardinal Piazza

Suor Maria Rosa, Superior of the Dominican Sisters

Dott. Luciano Palandri, General of the Armored Corp of the Guardians of the Finance

Dott. Nicola De Cristoforo, Police Commissioner of Venice

Dott.ssa Giovanna Nepi Scirè, Superintendent of Fine Arts and History of Venice

Dott. Gracco Crevato, Grand Chancellor of the Scuola di San Rocco

Dott. Silvio Fuso and *dott. Sandro Mescola*, Directors of Palazzo Fortuny

Dott.ssa Maria Teresa Muraro, Institute for Literature, Theatre and Melodrama of the Giorgio Cini Foundation

Dott. Philip Rylands, Deputy Director of the Peggy Guggenheim Collection

The authors wish to thank the owners of the following private gardens:
Angelica Alverà, Associazione Bocciofili, Loredana Balboni, Francesca Baldissera, Paola Barbini, Anna Barnabò, Maria Barozzi, Francesca and Maria Teresa Bastianello, Gino Bastianello, Sara Bellinato, Luciana Bennati, Renato Borsato, Brando Brandolini d'Adda, Elena e Margherita Calzavara, Francesca Candiani, Gabriella Cardazzo, Giuliano Carrettin, Annina e Renata Casellati, Enzo Cassetti, Enrica Cavenago, Fiorella Chiari, Elena Ciceri, Alberto Cosulich, Laura Crolle, Ottavio Croze, Cesare De Michelis, Francesca De Pol, Giuliana Di Thiene, Ucci Ferruzzi, Vittorio Fiorazzo, Joan Fitzgerald, Alberta Foscari, Ida Teresa Fullin, Grazia Gaggia, Chiara Ghetti, Walter Gobbetto, Antonietta and Maria Luisa Gradenigo, Umberto Graffi, Marinella Herion, Liselotte Höhs Manera, Lynn Lazzarini, Evelina Levi Broglio, Renato Levi Morenos, Nella Lopez y Royo, Maria Lucheschi, Adele Macchi, Umberto Marcello del Maino, Alessandra Mainardis, Paolo Marsoni, Franco Marzollo, Pippo Montanari, Giovanni Morelli, Agostino Nani Mocenigo, Lucio e Ruggero Orsoni, Patrizia Piva, Carlo Maria and Massimiliano Rocca, Conny and Natale Rusconi, Franca Sacerdoti, Carla Salmistrari, Michele and Vettor Sammartini, Flora Soldan, Rosetta Stangherlin, Maria Luisa Terra, Lidia Torzo, Sergio Uberti, Dario Ustino, Patricia Viganò Curtis.

The authors wish to thank the following individuals, in particular, for their generous help:
Donatella Asta, Elena Bassi, Maurizio Biraghi, Piero Breda, Vittoria de Buzzaccarini, Ugo Camerino, Porzia Casoni, Angela Churchill, Anna e Paolo Crovato, Vincenzo Fontana, Bianca Lanfranchi Strina, Gerolamo Marcello, Matilde Marcello, Carlo Montanaro, Don Antonio Niero, Lina Padoan Urban, Jasminska Pomorišac De Luigi, Nunu Reghini di Pontremoli, Maurizio Sammartini, Anna Tortorella, Giorgio Trani, Egle Trincanato, Francesca Zanuso and Ina Callegari of the Marciana National Library, Umberto Lo Cascio, Riccardo Manni, Urbano Pasquon of the Correr Library.

156

Bibliography

ALBERTI, LEON BATTISTA, *L'architettura. De re aedificatoria*, Milan, Il Polifilo, 1966, 2 vols.

ALVERÀ BORTOLOTTO, ANGELICA, *Storia della ceramica a Venezia: dagli albori alla fine della Repubblica*, Florence, Sansoni, 1981.

Ambiente scientifico veneziano tra Cinque e Seicento: testimonianze d'archivio, exhibiton catalog, Venice, Archivio di Stato, Jul. 27 – Oct. 6 1985, Venice, Archivio di Stato, 1985.

Architettura e utopia nella Venezia del Cinquecento, edited by Lionello Puppi, Milan, Electa, 1980.

ARETINO, PIETRO, *Lettere (1538)*, edited by Francesco Flora, Milan, Mondadori, 1960, 2 vols.

AZZI VISENTINI, MARGHERITA, *L'orto botanico di Padova e il giardino del Rinascimento*, Milan, Il Polifilo, 1984.

AZZI VISENTINI, MARGHERITA, 'Per un profilo del giardino a Venezia e nel Veneto', *Comunità*, Nov. 1985.

BALSTON, MICHAEL, *The Well-Furnished Garden*, London, M. Beazley, 1986.

Barocco europeo e barocco veneziano, edited by Vittore Branca, Florence, Sansoni, 1962.

BASALDELLA, FRANCESCO, *Giudecca: cenni storici*, Venice, F. Basaldella, 1983.

BASSI, ELENA, *Architettura del Sei e Settecento a Venezia*, Naples, Edizioni scientifiche italiane, 1962.

BASSI, ELENA, *Il Convento della Carità*, Vicenza, Centro internazionale di studi di architettura 'Andrea Palladio', 1971.

BASSI, ELENA, *Palazzi di Venezia: Admiranda urbis Venetae*, Venice, Stamperia di Venezia, 1976.

BATTILANA, MARILLA, *Scrittori inglesi a Venezia (1350-1950): antologia di testi in lingua originale*, Venice, Stamperia di Venezia, 1981.

BATTILANA, MARILLA, *Venezia sfondo e simbolo nella narrativa di Henry James*, Milan, Laboratorio delle arti, 1971.

BEARDSLEY, AUBREY, *The Story of Venus and Tannhäuser or 'Under the Hill': a Romantic Novel*, London Academy, New York, Martin, 1974.

BEARDSLEY, AUBREY, *Under the Hill and Other Essays in Prose and Verse*, Paddington, 1977.

BEIGBEDER, OLIVIER, *Lexique des symboles*, Geneva, 1969.

BELLAVITIS, GIORGIO; ROMANELLI, GIANDOMENICO, *Venezia*, Rome, Bari, Laterza, 1985.

BEMBO, PIETRO, *Lettere / di M. Pietro / Bembo / a principi et signori / et Suoi Famigliari, Amici Scritte, / divise in dodici libri*, Venetia, Giovanni Alberti, 1587.

Bissone, peote e galleggianti: addobbi e costumi per cortei e regate, edited by Giandomenico Romanelli and Filippo Pedrocco, Venice, Alfieri, 1980.

BISTORT, GIULIO, *Il Magistrato alle Pompe nella Repubblica di Venezia*, Bologna, Forni, 1969.

BLANC, CHARLES, *De Paris à Venise: notes au crayon*, Paris, Hachette, 1857.

BONFANTI, LICINIO, *L'isola della Giudecca*, Venice, Libreria Emiliana, 1930.

BONLINI, CARLO, *La gloria della poesia e della musica contenute nell'esatta notizia de' teatri della città di Venezia…*, Venice, Carlo Bonarigo Stampatore, 1730.

BOSCHINI, MARCO, *La carta del navegar pitoresco*, edited by Anna Pallucchini, Rome, Istituto per la collaborazione culturale, 1968.

BRANCA, VITTORE (editor), *Storia della civiltà veneziana, (Autunno del Medioevo e Rinascimento)*, Florence, Sansoni, 1979, vol. 3.

BROWN, HORATIO F., *Life in the Lagoons*, London, Rivingtons, 1904[4].

BRUSATIN, MANLIO, *Arte della meraviglia*, Turin, G. Einaudi, 1986.

BRUSATIN, MANLIO, 'Costruzione della campagna e dell'architettura del paesaggio', in *La città di Padova*, edited by C. Aymonino, Rome, 1970.

BRUSATIN, MANLIO, *Storia dei colori*, Turin, G. Einaudi, 1983[2].

BURCKHARDT, JACOB, *The Civilization of the Renaissance in Italy: an Essay*, London, Phaidon, 1960.

BURNETT, FRANCES HODGSON, *The Secret Garden*, New York, J. B. Lippincott, 1985.

CACCIAPAGLIA, GIACOMO, *Scrittori di lingua tedesca a Venezia dal XV secolo a oggi. Deutschsprachige Schriftsteller und Venedig von XV. Jahrhundert bis heute*, Venice, Stamperia di Venezia, 1985.

CALAS, NICOLAS; CALAS, ELENA, *The Peggy Guggenheim Collection of Modern Art*, New York, H.N. Abrams, 1960.

CALVESI, MAURIZIO, *Il sogno di Polifilo Prenestino*, Rome, Officina, 1980.

CANAL, MARTINO DA, *Les histoires de Venise*, reprint of 1275 edition, edited by Alberto Libertani, Florence, Leo S. Olschki, 1973.

CAPELLO, GIOVANNI BATTISTA, *Lessico farmaceutico-chimico contenente li rimedi più usati d'oggidì*, Venice, Antonio Graziosi, 1775[10].

CARLEVARIJS, LUCA, *Le Fabriche et Vedute di Venetia disegnate, poste in prospettiva et intagliate*, Venice, G.B. Finazzi, 1703.

CASANOVA, GIACOMO, *Istorie delle turbolenze della Polonia*, in Elena Bassi, *Palazzi di Venezia: Admiranda urbis Venetae*, Venice, Stamperia di Venezia, 1976.

CASANOVA DE SEINGALT, JACQUES, *Histoire de ma vie*, Wiesbaden, F.A. Brockhaus, Paris, Librairie Plon, 1960-1962, 12 vols.

CASOLA, PIETRO, *Canon Pietro Casola's Pilgrimage to Jerusalem in the Year 1494*, trad. M.M. Newett, Manchester (England), University Press, 1907.

CASSINI, GIOCONDO, *Piante e vedute prospettiche di Venezia (1479-1855)*, Venice, Stamperia di Venezia, 1982.

CECCHETTI, BARTOLOMEO, *Del giardino dei signori Borghi*, Venice, Naratovich, 1888.

CESSI, ROBERTO, *Un millennio di storia veneziana*, Venice, G. Poli, 1964.

CESSI, ROBERTO, *Le origini del ducato veneziano*, Naples, Morano, 1951.

CHEVALIER, JEAN; GHEERBRANT, ALAIN, *Dictionnaire des symboles*, Paris, R. Laffont, 1969.

CICOGNA, EMANUELE ANTONIO, *Delle inscrizioni veneziane raccolte e illustrate da…*, Venice, G. Orlandelli, 1824-1853, 7 vols.

CLARICI, PAOLO BARTOLOMEO, *Istoria e coltura delle piante… con un copioso Trattato degli agrumi*, Venice, Andrea Poletti, 1728.

Codex Publicorum. Codice del Piovego, edited by Bianca Lanfranchi Strina, Venice, Deputazione di storia patria per le Venezie, Comitato per la pubblicazione delle fonti relative alla storia di Venezia, 1985, vol. I.

COLE, TOBY (editor), *Venice: a Portable Reader*, Westport, L. Hill, 1979.

COLLIER, PETER, *Mosaici proustiani: Venezia nelle 'Ricerche'*, Bologna, Il Mulino, 1986.

COLONNA, FRANCESCO, *Hypnerotomachia Poliphili*, reprint of the 1499 edition, edited by G.Pozzi and L.A.Ciapponi, Padua, Antenore, 1980, 2 vols.

COLONNA, FRANCESCO, *Hypnerotomachia Poliphili, ubi hu / mana omnia non nisisomnium / esse docet. Atque obiter / plurima scitu sane / quam digna con / memorat*, Farnborough, Hants, Gregg Int., 1969.

COMBATTI, BERNARDO; COMBATTI, GAETANO; BERLAN, FRANCESCO, *Nuova planimetria della città di Venezia divisa in venti tavole*, Venice, P. Naratovich, 1846.

COMMYNES, PHILIPPE DE, *Les memoires*, reprint of 1524 edition, edited by M.C. Daviso di Charvesod, Turin, Einaudi, 1960.

CORNARO, ALVISE, *Progetto di teatro… (1560)*, in Nicola Mangini, *I teatri di Venezia*, Milan, Mursia, 1974.

CORNER, FLAMINIO, *Notizie storiche delle chiese e monasteri di Venezia e di Torcello*, Padua, Stamperia del Seminario, G. Manfrè, 1758.

CRIVELLARI, DOMENICO, *Venezia*, Milan, Electa, 1982.

DAMERINI, GINO, *La Ca' Grande dei Cappello e dei Malipiero di S. Samuele ora Barnabò*, Venice, Edizioni del Grifone, 1962.

DAMERINI, GINO, *D'Annunzio a Venezia*, Verona, Mondadori, 1943.

DAMERINI, GINO, *Giardini di Venezia*, Bologna, Zanichelli, 1931.

DAMERINI, GINO, *Giardini sulla laguna*, Bologna, 1927.

DAMERINI, GINO, 'Un teatro per la *Talanta* dell'Aretino', in *Il dramma*, no. 306 (1962).

DA MOSTO, ANDREA, *I dogi di Venezia nella vita pubblica e privata*, Florence, A. Martello, 1966.

D'ANNUNZIO, GABRIELE, *Altri taccuini*, edited by Enrica Bianchetti, Verona, Mondadori, 1976.

D'ANNUNZIO, GABRIELE, *Il fuoco*, Milan, F.lli Treves, 1913.

D'ANNUNZIO, GABRIELE, *La Leda senza cigno: racconto seguito da una 'Licenza'*, Milan, Mondadori, 1976.

D'ANNUNZIO GABRIELE, *Notturno*, Milan, Mondadori, 1983.

D'ANNUNZIO, GABRIELE, *Taccuini*, edited by Enrica Bianchetti and Roberto Forcella, Verona, Mondadori, 1965.

DAVIS, JAMES C., *The Decline of the Venetian Nobility as a Ruling Class*, Baltimore, J. Hopkins, 1962.

DETIENNE, MARCEL, *I giardini di Adone*, Turin, G. Einaudi, 1975.

DE VISIANI, ROBERTO, *Delle benemerenze de' Veneti nella botanica: discorso letto nella Sala de' Pregadi del Palazzo Ducale di Venezia nel dì 30 maggio 1854*, Venice, Cecchini, 1854.

DE VISIANI, ROBERTO, *Delle origini ed anzianità dell'Orto botanico di Padova*, Venice, Merlo, 1839.

Dietro i palazzi: tre secoli di architettura minore a Venezia (1492-1803), edited by Giorgio Gianighian and Paola Pavanini, Venice, Arsenale Editrice, 1984.

The Eastern Carpet in the Western World from the 15th to the 17th Century, edited by Donald King and David Sylvester, exhition catalog, London, Hayward Gallery, 20 May-10 July 1983, London, Art Council of Great Britain, 1983.

EDEN, FRANCIS, *A Garden in Venice*, London, Contry Life & George Newnes, 1903.

FARIELLO, FRANCESCO, *Architettura dei giardini*, Rome, Edizioni dell'Ateneo, Scipioni, 1985.

FENAROLI, LUIGI; GAMBI, GERMANO, *Alberi: dendroflora italica*, Trento, Museo Tridentino di scienze naturali, 1976.

FILARETE, [Antonio Averlino], *Treatise on Architecture*, trad. J. Spencer, New Haven, Yale University Press, 1965, 2 vols.

FONTANA, GIAN JACOPO, *I principali palazzi di Venezia*, Venice, Scarbellina, n.d.

FOSCARI, ANTONIO; TAFURI, MANFREDO, *L'armonia e i conflitti: la chiesa di San Francesco della Vigna nella Venezia del '500*, Turin, G. Einaudi, 1983.

FRANCO, NICOLÒ, *La Philena*, in Pompeo Molmenti, *La storia di Venezia nella vita privata dalle origini alla caduta della Repubblica*, Bergamo, Istituto italiano d'arti grafiche, 1922-1927, 3 vols.

GARDANI, DANTE LUIGI, *L'Opera Pia Zuane Conterini (1380-1980): sei secoli al servizio del prossimo*, Venice, La Tipografia, 1980.

GASPARETTO, ASTONE, *Il vetro di Murano dalle origini a oggi*, Venice, N. Pozza, 1958.

GASPERONI, DOMENICO, *Artiglieria veneta dedicata al ser.mo principe Paolo Renier*, Venice, Biblioteca del Museo Correr, 1779 (ms cod. Cicogna, no. 3701, 3708).

GERA, FRANCESCO, *I principali giardini di Venezia*, Venice, Antonelli, 1847.

Giardini italiani, edited by Luca Pietromarchi, Milan, Fabbri, 1987.

Il giardino d'Europa: Pratolino come modello nella cultura europea, catalog edited by Alessandro Vezzosi, Milan, Mazzotta, 1986.

Il giardino romantico e Jappelli, edited by Paola Bussadori and Renato Roverato, exhibition catalog, Padua, Sala della Gran Guardia, 5-27 Nov. 1983, Padua, Antoniano, 1983.

GOLDONI, CARLO, *Memorie: scritte dal medesimo per l'istoria della sua vita e del suo teatro*, Milan, Sonzogno, 1915.

GRADENIGO, PIETRO, *Commemoriali di Pietro Gradenigo*, Venice, Biblioteca del Museo Correr, [1702] (ms Gradenigo Dolfin, no. 200), vol. 8.

GRAMIGNA, SILVIA; PERISSA, ANNALISA, *Scuole di arti, mestieri e devozione a Venezia*, Venice, Arsenale Editrice, 1981.

GUSSOW, ALAN, 'Images from my Garden', *Country Journal*, (May 1983).

HOFMANNSTHAL, HUGO VON, *Andrea o i ricongiunti*, Milan, Adelphi, 1984⁵.

HOUSSAYE, ARSÈNE, *Voyages humoristiques: Amsterdam, Paris, Venise*, Paris, L. Hachette, 1856.

HOWELLS, WILLIAM D., *Venetian Life*, Lipsia, Tauchnitz, 1931².

HUNT, JOHN DIXON, *Garden and Grove: the Italian Renaissance Garden in the English Imagination (1600-1750)*, London, Melbourne, J.M. Dent & Sons, 1986.

HUNT, JOHN DIXON, 'L'idea di un giardino nel bel mezzo del mare', *Rassegna*, vol. 3, no. 8 (Oct. 1981).

Interpretazioni veneziane: studi di storia dell'arte in onore di Michelangelo Muraro, edited by David Rosand, Venice, Arsenale Editrice, 1984.

L'Italie septentrionale vue par les grands écrivains et les voyageurs célèbres: le Piémont, Milan, Venise, Florence, l'Ombrie, Paris, Mercure de France, 1913.

IVANOVICH, CRISTOFORO, *Minerva al tavolino*, Venice, N. Pezzana, 1681.

JAMES, HENRY, *The Aspern Papers and The Turn of the Screw*, Harmondesworth (Great Britain), Penguin Books, 1984.

JAMES, HENRY, *Italian Hours*, New York, Grove Press, 1959.

JASSEO, NICANDRO, [Azevedo], *Venetae Urbae descriptio*, Venice, Tipografia ex Zattiano, 1780.

KIRCHER, ATHANASIUS, *Athanasii Kircheri e Soc. Jesu Turris Babel, sive Archontologia qua primo Priscorum post diluvium hominum vita, mores rerumque gestarum magnitudo, secundo Turris fabrica civitatumque exstructio, confusio linguarum...*, Amstelodami, ex officina Janssonio-Waebergiana, 1679.

LANE, FREDERIC C., *Storia di Venezia*, Turin, G. Einaudi, 1978.

La letteratura e i giardini, preecedings of the international studies convention, Garda (VR), 2-5 Oct. 1985, Florence, Leo S. Olschki, 1987.

LEVI D'ANCONA, MIRELLA, *The Garden of the Renaissance: Botanical Symbolism in Italian, Painting*, Florence, Leo S. Olschki, 1977.

LEWIS, C.S., *The Allegory of Love: a Study in Medieval Tradition*, London, Oxford, New York, 1972.

LINKS, J.G., *Venice for Pleasure*, London, The Bodley Head, 1966.

LONGHI, ROBERTO, *Viatico per cinque secoli di pittura veneziana*, Florence, Sansoni, 1952.

LORENZETTI, GIULIO, *Venezia e il suo estuario: guida storico-artistica*, Rome, Istituto poligrafico dello Stato, Libreria dello Stato, 1956².

LOVELL, MARGARETTA M. (editor), *Venice: the American View 1860-1920*, San Francisco, The Fine Arts Museums, 1984, exhibition catalog.

LOVISA, DOMENICO, *Il Gran Teatro di Venezia, ovvero Raccolta delle principali vedute e pitture che in essa si contengono*, Venice, 1720.

LUCAS, E.V., *A Wanderer in Venice*, New York, Mac Millan, 1914.

159

LURÇAT, JEAN, *Le bestiaire de la tapisserie du Moyen Age*, Ginevra, Paris, Cailler, 1947.

MADER, GÜNTER; NEUBERT-MADER, LEILA G., *Giardini all'italiana*, Milan, Rizzoli, 1987.

MANGINI, NICOLA, *I teatri di Venezia*, Milan, Mursia, 1974.

MANIGLIO CALCAGNO, ANNALISA, *Architettura del paesaggio*, Bologna, 1983.

MANN, THOMAS, *La morte a Venezia*, Turin, G. Einaudi, 1969[6].

MARCELLO, ALESSANDRO, *Divagazioni botaniche: la flora di Venezia*, in *Ateneo Veneto*, CXLIII, vol. 136, no. 1 (Jan.-June 1952).

MARCELLO, ALESSANDRO, *La flora urbica di Venezia*, in *Memorie di biogeografia adriatica*, Venice, 1973-1974, vol. 9.

MARCELLO, ALESSANDRO, *Piante e bioclima a Venezia*, in *Minerva medica*, XLIII, vol. 2, no. 79 (1 Oct. 1952).

MARCELLO, ALESSANDRO, *Sulla vegetazione spontanea delle Venezie*, in *Ateneo Veneto*, CXLVIII, vol. 141, no. 2 (July-Dec. 1957).

MARCELLO, ALESSANDRO; PADOAN, MARIO, 'I giardini di Venezia: aspetti urbanistici e botanici', in *Atti dell'Istituto veneto di scienze, lettere ed arti: Classe di scienze matematiche e naturali*, vol. 132 (1973-1974).

MARCHIORI, GIUSEPPE; BERENGO GARDIN, GIANNI; *I Cadorin*, Florence, Alinari, 1968.

MARETTO, PAOLO, *La casa veneziana nella storia della città dalle origini all'Ottocento*, Venice, Marsilio, 1986.

MARSILI, GIOVANNI, *Notizie inedite scritte da G. Marsili: dei patrizi veneti dotti nella cognizione delle piante e dei loro orti botanici*, Padua, 1840.

MASSON, GIORGINA, *Italian Gardens*, London, Antique Collectors' Club, 1987.

MATTIOLI, PIER ANDREA, *Discorsi nelli sei libri di Dioscoride*, Venice, 1568.

MC ANDREW, JOHN, *Venetian Architecture of the Early Renaissance*, Cambridge (MA), London, MIT, 1980.

MC CARTHY, MARY, *Venice Observed*, New York, Harvest Book, Harcout, Brace & World, 1963.

MICHIEL, PIER ANTONIO, *I cinque libri di piante*, edited by E. De Toni, Venice, 1940.

MOLMENTI, POMPEO, 'Le prime rappresentazioni teatrali a Venezia', *La rassegna nazionale*, vol. 150 (1906).

MOLMENTI, POMPEO, *La storia di Venezia nella vita privata dalle origini alla caduta della Repubblica*, Bergamo, Istituto italiano d'arti grafiche, 1922-1927[6], 3 vols.

MONTAIGNE, MICHEL DE, *Viaggio in Italia (1580-1581)*, translated by Irene Riboli, Milan, Bompiani, 1942.

MORATO, FULVIO PELLEGRINO, *Del signi / ficato de colori / e de mazzolli / : operetta di...*, Vinegia, Francesco de Leno, 1559.

MORRIS, JAMES, *The Venetian Empire: a Sea Voyage*, London, Boston, Faber and Faber, 1980.

MORRIS, JAMES, *Venice*, London, Faber and Faber, 1960.

MOSCHINI, GIANNANTONIO, *Ragguaglio delle cose notabili nella Chiesa e nel Seminario Patriarcale di S. Maria della Salute in Venezia*, Venice, Tipografia di Alvisopoli, 1819.

Mostra storica della laguna veneta, exhibition catalog, Venice, Palazzo Grassi 11 July-27 Sept. 1970, Venice, Stamperia di Venezia, 1970.

MURARO, MICHELANGELO, *Civiltà delle ville venete*, Udine, Magnus, 1986.

MURARO, MICHELANGELO, *La vita nelle pietre: sculture marciane e civiltà veneziana del Duecento*, Venice, Arsenale Editrice, 1985.

MURARO, MICHELANGELO; GRABAR ANDRÉ, *Les trésor de Venise*, Geneva, Skira, 1963.

MUSATTI, EUGENIO, *La donna in Venezia*, Bologna, Forni, 1975.

NEGRI, GIOVANNI, *Erbario figurato: con speciale riguardo alle piante medicinali*, Milan, Hoepli, 1920.

NISSATTI, GIUSEPPE, pseud. [Giuseppe Tassini], *Aneddoti storici veneziani*, Venice, Filippi, 1965[2].

NORWICH, JOHN JULIUS, *Venice: the Greatness and the Fall*, London, A. Lane, 1981, 2 vols.

PADOAN URBAN, LINA, 'Il carnevale veneziano', in *Storia della cultura veneta dalla Controriforma alla fine della Repubblica*, vol. 1 *(Il Settecento)*, Venice, N. Pozza, 1985, vol. 5.

PADOAN URBAN, LINA (editor), *Il carnevale veneziano nelle maschere incise da Francesco Bertelli*, Milan, Il Polifilo, 1986.

PADOAN URBAN, LINA, 'Le Compagnie della Calza: edonismo e cultura al servizio della politica', *Quaderni veneti*, no. 6 (1987).

PADOAN URBAN, LINA, 'Feste ufficiali e trattamenti privati', in *Storia della cultura veneta della Controriforma alla fine della Repubblica*, vol. 4, vol. 1 *(Il Seicento)*, Venice, N. Pozza, 1983.

PAGANUZZI, GIOVANNI BATTISTA, *Iconografia delle trenta parrocchie di Venezia*, Venice, 1821.

PALLADIO, ANDREA, *I quattro libri dell'architettura*, Venice, Domenico de' Franceschi, 1570.

PAOLETTI, ERMOLAO, *Il fiore di Venezia*, Venice, Tipografia Fontana, 1839.

PAOLETTI, PIETRO, *L'architettura e la scultura del Rinascimento in Venezia*, Venice, 1893.

PASSI, MARCO CELIO, *Il Gran Priorato di Lombardia e Venezia: del Sovrano Militare Ordine Ospedaliero di San Giovanni di Gerusalemme, di Rodi, di Malta*, Venice, Gran Priorato, 1983.

PAULY, CHARLOTTE ELFRIEDE, *Der venezianische Lustgarten*, Strasbourg, Heitz & Mündel, 1916.

PAVANELLO, ITALO (editor), *I catasti storici di Venezia 1808-1913*, Rome, Officina, 1981.

PEROCCO, GUIDO; SALVADORI, ANTONIO, *Civiltà di Venezia*, Venice, Stamperia di Venezia, 1973, 3 vols.

PERSIO, ANTONIO, *Trattato dei portamenti della Signoria di Venetia verso la Santa Chiesa (1607)*, in

Nicola Mangini, *I teatri di Venezia*, Milan, Mursia, 1974.

PIAMONTE, GIANNINA, *Venezia vista dall'acqua: guida dei rii di Venezia e delle isole*, Venice, Stamperia di Venezia, 1966.

PIGUET, PHILIPPE, *Monet et Venise*, Paris, Herscher, 1986.

PRAZ, MARIO, *Il giardino dei sensi: studi sul manierismo e il barocco*, Milan, Mondadori, 1975.

PREST, JOHN, *The Garden of Eden: the Botanic Garden and the Recreation of Paradise*, New Haven, London, 1981.

PROUST, MARCEL, *Alla ricerca del tempo perduto*, edited by Franco Fortini, vol. 6 (*La fuggitiva*), Turin, G. Einaudi, 1965.

PUPPI, LIONELLO, 'I giardini veneziani del Rinascimento', *Il veltro*, vol. 22, nos. 3-4 (1978).

PUPPI, LIONELLO (editor), *Palladio a Venezia*, Florence, Sansoni, 1982.

PUPPI, LIONELLO, 'Venezia come Gerusalemme nella cultura figurativa del Rinascimento', in *La città italiana del Rinascimento fra utopia e realtà*, edited by August Buck and Bodo Guthmiller, Venice, Centro tedesco di studi veneziani, 1984 (*Quaderni*, no. 27).

QUADRI, ANTONIO, *Il Canal Grande di Venezia*, Venice, 1838.

QUADRI, ANTONIO, *Huit jours à Venise*, Venice, A. Bazzarini, 1838[6].

RÉGNIER, HENRI DE, *Esquisses vénitiennes*, Paris, Collection de l'Art décoratif, 1906.

RENIER MICHIEL, GIUSTINA, *Origine delle feste veneziane*, Torino, Ghiringhelli & Reycend bros., 1830, 6 vols.

RIDOLFI, CARLO, *Le meraviglie dell'arte ovvero le vite degli illustri pittori Veneti e dello Stato*, edited by Detlev von Hadeln, Berlin, 1914-1921, 2 vols.

RIZZI, ALBERTO, *Scultura esterna a Venezia: corpus delle sculture erratiche all'aperto di Venezia e della sua laguna*, Venice, Stamperia di Venezia, 1987.

RIZZI, ALBERTO, *Vere da pozzo di Venezia: i puteali pubblici di Venezia e della sua laguna*, Venice, Stamperia di Venezia, 1981.

RIZZI, ALDO, *Luca Carlevarijs*, Venice, Alfieri, 1967.

ROLFE, FREDERICK, *Il desiderio e la ricerca del tutto: un romanzo di Venezia moderna*, Milan, Longanesi, 1963.

ROMANELLI, GIANDOMENICO, *Venezia Ottocento: Materiali per una storia architettonica e urbanistica della città nel secolo XIX*, Rome, Officina, 1977.

ROSS, JAMES BRUCE, *Gasparo Contarini and His Friends*, in *Studies in the Renaissance*, 1970, vol. 17.

RUSKIN, JOHN, *Ruskin Today*, edited by Kenneth Clark, Harmondsworth (England), Penguin Books, 1982.

RUSKIN, JOHN, *The Stones of Venice*, edited by Jan Morris, Boston, Toronto, Little, Brown and Co., 1981.

SABELLICO, MARC'ANTONIO, *Del sito di Venezia città (1502)*, edited by G. Meneghetti, Venice, Stamperia già Zanetti, 1957.

SACCARDO, PIETRO ANTONIO, 'Della prima istituzione degli orti botanici e delle cattedre dei semplici in Italia', in *Nuovo giornale botanico italiano*, vol. 23 (1891).

SAINT DIDIER, LINAJON DE, *La ville et la Republique de Venise*, Paris, 1680.

SANSOVINO, FRANCESCO, *Venetia città nobilissima et singolare con le aggiunte di Giustiniano Martinoni*, Venice, Stefano Curti, 1663.

SANUDO, MARIN (il Giovane), *De origine, situ et magistratibus urbis Venetae, ovvero La città di Venezia (1493-1530)*, edited by Angela Caracciolo Aricò, Milan, Istituto editoriale cisalpino-goliardica, 1980.

SCATTOLIN, GIORGIA, *Le case-fondaco sul Canal Grande*, Venice, G. Scattolin, 1961.

SCHULZ, JUERGEN, *The Printed Plans and Panoramic Views of Venice (1486-1797)*, Florence, Leo S. Olschki, 1970.

SCHWARZ, ANGELO (editor), *Per una storia della farmacia e del farmacista in Italia: Venezia e Veneto*, Bologna, Skema, 1981.

SCOTO, FRANCESCO, *Itinerario / overo / nova descrittione / di viaggi principali / d'Italia / di Francesco Scoto / aggiontavi in quest'ultima impressione / le descrittioni / di Udine…*, Venetia, Gio' Pietro Brigonci, 1665.

SELINCOURT, BERYL DE; HENDERSON, MAY STINGE, *Venice*, New York, Dodd, Mead, 1907.

SELVATICO, PIETRO, *Lettere alla Sig.ra M.B.B.*, Padua, Bettoni, 1815.

SELVATICO, PIETRO, *Sulla architettura e sulla scultura in Venezia dal Medioevo sino ai nostri giorni: studi di P. Selvatico per servire di guida estetica*, Venice, P. Ripamonti Carpano, 1847.

SHAW-KENNEDY, RONALD, *Venice Rediscovered*, Filadelphia, Art Alliance Press, 1978.

SYMONDS, JOHN ADDINGTON, *New Italian Sketches*, Lipsia, Tauchnitz, 1884.

SYMONS, ARTHUR J.A., *The Quest for Corvo*, London, The Folio Society, 1952.

TAFURI, MANFREDO, *Venezia e il Rinascimento: religione, scienza, architettura*, Turin, G. Einaudi, 1985.

TAGLIOLINI, ALESSANDRO, *Storia del giardino italiano. Gli artisti, l'invenzione, le forme dall'antichità al XIX secolo*, Florence, GEF, 1988.

TAMASSIA MAZZAROTTO, BIANCA, *Le feste veneziane: i giochi popolari, le cerimonie religiose e di governo illustrate da Gabriel Bella*, Florence, Sansoni, 1980[2].

TASSINARI, GIUSEPPE, *Manuale dell'agronomo*, edited by Boris Carlo Fischetti, Rome, REDA, 19765.

TASSINI, GIUSEPPE, *Cenni storici e leggi circa il libertinaggio in Venezia dal secolo decimoquarto alla caduta della Repubblica*, Venice, Filippi, 1968.

TASSINI, GIUSEPPE, *Curiosità veneziane, ovvero Origini delle denominazioni stradali*, edited by Lino Moretti,

161

Venice, Filippi, 1964.

TASSINI, GIUSEPPE, *Edifici di Venezia distrutti o volti ad altro uso da quello a cui furono in origine destinati*, Venice, Filippi, 1969.

TASSINI, GIUSEPPE, *Feste, spettacoli, divertimenti e piaceri degli antichi veneziani*, Venice, Filippi, 1961.

I teatri pubblici di Venezia (secoli XVII-XVIII), edited by Ludovico Zorzi, Maria Teresa Muraro, Gianfranco Prato, Elvi Zorzi, exhibition catalog, Venice, La Biennale, XXX International Theatre Festival, 1971.

TEMANZA, TOMASO, *Vite di più celebri architetti e scultori veneziani che fiorirono nel secolo decimosesto*, Venice, Stamperia C. Polese, 1778.

TEMANZA, TOMASO, *Zibaldone (1738-1778)*, edited by Nicola Ivanoff, Venice, Rome, Istituto per la collaborazione culturale, 1963.

THACKER, CHRISTOPHER, *The History of Gardens*, London, Croom Helm, 1979.

TRINCANATO, EGLE RENATA, *Venezia minore*, with a chapter by Agnoldomenico Pica, Venice, Filippi, 1948.

TWAIN, MARK, *Innocents Abroad, or The New Pilgrim's Progress*, New York, G. Wells, 1922, 2 vols.

Umanesimo europeo e Umanesimo veneziano, edited by Vittore Branca, Florence, Sansoni, 1963.

VASARI, GIORGIO, *Opere*, edited by G. Milanesi, Florence, Sansoni, 1881.

VASARI, GIORGIO, *Le vite de' più eccellenti pittori, scultori e architettori*, Florence, A. Salani, 1927-1932, 7 vols.

VAUDOYER, JEAN-LOUIS, *Les délices de l'Italie*, Paris, Plon-Nourrit, [1924][9].

VECELLIO, TIZIANO, *Le lettere*, Belluno, Magnifica Comunità di Cadore, 1977.

Venezia e Bisanzio: Venezia, exhibition catalog, Venice, Doges Palace, 8 June-30 Sept. 1974, Milan, Electa, 1974.

Venezia e la peste: 1348-1797, Venice, Marsilio, 1979, file no. 141 by Jasminka Pomorišac De Luigi, p. 330.

Venezia e l'Oriente tra tardo Medioevo e Rinascimento, edited by Agostino Pertusi, Florence, Sansoni, 1966.

Venezia e lo spazio scenico, exhibition catalog, Venice, Palazzo Grassi, 6 Oct.-4 Nov. 1979, Venice, La Biennale di Venezia, 1979.

Venezia: forma urbis: il fotopiano a colori del centro storico in scala 1:500, Venice, Comune di Venezia, Marsilio, 1985.

Venezia nelle letterature moderne, edited by Carlo Pellegrini, preeedings of the first convention of the International Association of Compared Literature, Venice, 25-30 Sept. 1955, Venice, Rome, Istituto per la collaborazione culturale, 1971.

Venezia nell'Ottocento: immagini e mito, edited by Giuseppe Pavanello and Giandomenico Romanelli, exhibition catalog, Milan, Electa, 1983.

Venezia piante e vedute, edited by Giandomenico Romanelli and Susanna Biadene, exhibition catalog

of *Fondo cartografico a stampa*, Venice, Museo Correr, April 1982, supplement of *Bollettino dei Musei civici veneziani*, Venice, Comune di Venezia, 1982.

Le Venezie possibili: da Palladio a Le Corbusier, edited by Lionello Puppi and Giandomenico Romanelli, exhibition catalog, Venice, Ala Napoleonica, Museo Correr, May-July 1985, Milan, Electa, 1985.

Venise au temps des galères, Paris, Hachette, 1968.

VENTURI, LIONELLO, *La Compagnia della Calza (sec. XV-XVI)*, Venice, Filippi, 1983.

VERCELLONI, MATTEO, *Il paradiso terrestre: viaggio tra i manufatti del giardino dell'uomo*, Milan, Jaca Book, 1986.

Viaggiatori stranieri a Venezia, catalog of the Angelo Tursi collection at the Biblioteca Nazionale Marciana of Venice, Moncalieri, Centro interuniversitario di ricerche sul viaggio in Italia, 1979, supplement of *Bollettino del CIRVI*, no. 1.

VIANELLO, RICCARDO (editor), *Una gemma di Venezia: la Giudecca*, Venice, Tipografia Veneta, 1966.

VISCEGLIA, ENZO, *Guida toponomastica di Venezia, Lido, Murano*, Rome, Istituto geografico Visceglia, [1970].

VIVIAN, FRANCES, *Il console Smith: mercante e collezionista*, Venice, N. Pozza, 1971.

VOLTOLINA, GINO, *Le antiche vere da pozzo veneziane*, Venice, Fantoni libri d'arte, 1981.

WHITTICK, ARNOLD (editor), *Ruskin's Venice*, London, G. Godwin, 1976.

WILSON, EDWARD D., 'The Right Place', in *Biophilia*, Harward, University Press, 1984.

YAMS, E., *A History of Gardens and Gardening*, London, Thacker-Crom Helm, 1971.

ZANOTTO, FRANCESCO, *Nuovissima guida di Venezia e delle isole della sua laguna*, Venice, G. Brizeghel, 1865.

ZANOTTO, FRANCESCO, *Venezia e le sue lagune*, Venice, 1847.

ZENDRINI, B., *Memorie storiche dello stato antico e moderno delle lagune di Venezia e di que' fiumi che restarono divertiti per la conservazione delle medesime*, Padua, 1811.

ZORZI, ALVISE, *Venezia scomparsa*, Milan, Electa, 1984[2].

ZUCCHETTA, GIANPIETRO, *I rii di Venezia: la storia degli ultimi tre secoli*, Venice, Helvetia, Foligraf, 1985.

162

Index of Names and Places

Page numbers of illustrations are indicated in **boldface** *type*

Abbazia della Misericordia **23**, **97**
Accademia dei Nobili e di Botanica 88
Accademia (pensione) 125
Altieri (garden) 128, **130**
Altieri, Emilio 128
Altieri, Gasparo 130
Alverà 24
Amadio, Andrea 85
Antonello da Messina 26
Arcimboldo 73
Aretino, Pietro 20, 57, 80, 92, 98, 102, 104, 125
Armenian College (Ca' Zenobio) **14**, **42**, 64, **132-133**, **144**, 149
Armitage, Kenneth 68
Arp, Jean 68
Augustine, Saint 15

Balbi Valier **56**, 68, **124**
Balboni **103**
Baldissera Adolfo **126-127**
Barbarigo (villa) 122
Barbarigo, Agostino 73
Barbaro (palazzo) **96**, **123**
Barbaro, Daniele 85
Barnabò 73, 76, **77**, **80**
Barozzi 34, **43**
Basadonna Recanati 32
Bassi, Elena 80
Bastianello (Businello) 20
Battistello 73
Beardsley, Aubrey 152
Bellinato 42, **102**
Bellini, Giovanni 26, 88
Bembo, Bernardo 20
Bembo, Pietro 20
Bennati 24, 125
Bernardo 64
Bolani, Domenico 98
Bonazza, Tommaso 76

Boschini, Marco 72
Brandolini d'Adda or Brandolin (Giustiniani) 26, 31, 56, 57, **99**, **100-101**, 145, 146, 148
Briati, Giuseppe 114, 136
Brown, Horatio 96,
Brown, Lancelot (Capability) 107
Brunswick, duke of 118
Businelli 73

Ca' Corner della Regina 68
Ca' Dario **112**, 137
Ca' Dolfin **64**
Ca' Leon 17, **32**, **33**, 56, 104
Ca' Tron **69**
Ca' Venier dei Leoni *see* Guggenheim
Ca' Zenobio *see* Armenian College
Cadorin, abbot 57
Calmo, Andrea 90
Calzavara 24, **28-29**, **39**
Canal, Martino da 24, 98
Cappello 44, **74-75**, 134, **135**, 137
Cappello Malipiero *see* Barnabò
Carlevarijs, Luca 64, **68**
Carmelite (Barefoot) Friars 91, **153**
Carpaccio, Vittore 26, 88
Casa Frollo 16, **38**
Casanova, Giacomo 17, 131, 134
Casati Stampa, Luisa 42
Casino degli Spiriti *see* Contarini dal Zaffo
Casola, Pietro 34
Cassiodorus 48
Cavazza, Gerolamo 57
Chigi, Costanza 128
Cicogna, Emanuele 72, 114
Cima da Conegliano 88
Cipriani **86-87**, 88, **89**
Clarici, Paolo Bartolomeo 62, 64, 80, 106, 107
Colonna, Francesco 119, 122, 124,

136, 152
Colonna, Vittoria 138
Combatti, Bernardo and Gaetano 20, 22, 31
Company of the stockings 124, 125
Condulmer 134
Contarini dal Zaffo **76**, 80, 136
Contarini Iron Gate **27**
Contarini, former palazzo **49**, **93**, **98**, **122**
Contarini, Gaspare 138
Contarini, Tomaso 92, 138
Cornaro 55
Cornaro, Alvise 118, 119
Cornaro, Benedetto 20
Cornaro, monsignor 73
Cosulich 24, **60-61**
Council of Ten 124
Crivelli, Carlo 88
Croce (church) 104
Curtis 96

D'Annunzio 15, 20, 25, 31, 32, 34, 38, 42, 43, 73, 76, 80, 85, 90, 92, 96, 113, 114, 130, 131, 134, 137, 138, 148
Damerini, Gino 20
Dandolo (palazzo) 85
Dandolo, Andrea 55, 85
De' Barbari, Jacopo **16**, 38
De Kooning, Willem 68
De' Medici, Giovanni 20
De Visiani, Roberto 85, 149
Della Casa, monsignor Giovanni 20
Delle Greche, Domenico 85
Di Thiene **149**
Dioscorides 85
Donà dalle Rose 56
Donati 73
Duncan, Isidora 42
Duse, Eleonora 42

Eden, former 17, **21**
Eden, Francis 17, 102, 105, 106
Erizzo, Francesco 72
Ernst, Max 68
Everlasting (company of the stockings) 124, 125
Ezechiel 55

Faithful (company of the stockings) 124
Falier **115**
Flamming Ones (company of the stockings) 124, 128
Fiorazzo 24
Forlani, Paolo 17, 20
Fortuny, Mariano 119
Foscari (doge) 96
Foscari, Alberta 70
Foscarini (garden) 73
Foscarini, Luigi 73
Francis II, Emperor of Austria 90
Franco, Nicolò 131
Frederick IV, king of Denmark 38
Fullin 30, **35**, **125**

Gardeners (company of the stockings) 124
Gaspari, Gian Giacomo 64
Gasperoni, Domenico 118
Giacometti, Alberto 68
Giannotti, Donato 20
Giustinian or Giustiniani *see* Brandolini
Goldoni, Carlo 30, 130
Gonzaga, Federico 85
Gonzales, Julio 68
Gozzi 56, **58**, **59**, **106**
Gradenigo 22, 24, 38, 43, 91, 134, 137
Gradenigo Dolfin 134
Grimani (Vendramin Calergi) 25, 31, **66-67**, 68, 70
Gritti 55
Gualtieri 85
Guardi, Francesco 76
Guggenheim, Collezione (Ca' Venier dei Leoni) **65**, 68, 72, **73**, **109**, 148

Herion 16, **22**, **25**
Hennessy, Timothy 138
Hofmannsthal, Hugo von 34
Howells, William D. 32, 44, 48, 114, 146, 148

Immortali (company of the stockings) 85
Isaiah 55
Ivanovich, Cristoforo 118, 137

James, Henry 6, 10, 43, 44, 48, 55, 72, 96
Joseph II, king of Germany 131

Knights of Malta 91

Kolb, Antony 16

Layard, lady 17
Lazzarini 26, **107**
Levi d'Ancona, Mariella 152
Levi-Morenos, Renato **48**, 68, **70**, 125
Lowry, Malcom 11
Lucas, E.V. 15, 68, 124
Lucheschi **63**, 64
Luke 148

Mangini, Nicola 119
Marcello, Alessandro 91, 118
Marini, Marino 68
Market Gardeners (company of the stockings) 124
Martinoni, Giustiniano 57, 58, 70, 73, 130
Massari 134
Maximilian II, king of Poland 73
Michiel, Antonio 85, 88
Minotto **44**, **147**
Mocenigo 24, 55, **116-117**, 138
Mocenigo Casagrande **131**
Mocenigo Marcello 88
Mocenigo Marcello, Loredana 85, 88
Modest (company of the stockings) 124
Molin (palazzo) 38
Molin, Bianca 57
Molin, Leonardo 57
Molmenti, Pompeo 131
Moore, Henry 68
Morosini 72
Morosini del Giardin 70, **71**, 72, **81**
Morosini-Gattemburg 72

Nacht, noble 56
Nani (palazzo) 85
Nardi, Jacopo 20, 57

Ospedale Umberto I 91
Orsoni **31**, **94-95**, 98
Orto dei Semplici 91

Padovan, Mario 91
Pagan, Matteo 17
Paganuzzi, Giovan Battista 90
Palladio, Andrea 42, 72, 73, 128
Paolozzi, Eduardo 68
Paradiso 124
Patarol (garden) 9, **90**
Patarol, Francesco 88
Patarol, Lorenzo 88
Patriarchal Seminary 31, **36-37**, 145
Pellegrini **152**
Persio, Antonio 128
Piovego 85
Pisani (villa) 122
Pliny 85, 146
Polignac 68
Poliphilus 119, 122, 149, 152
Pomorišac De Luigi, Jasminka 136

Poor Clares 104, **105**
Priscicane 57
Proust, Marcel 113

Radnor, lady 105
Raverti, Matteo 26
Régnier, Henry de 22, 30, 38, 102, 114, 137, 138
Ridolfi, Carlo 72, 73
Rinio, Benedetto 85
Rocca 42, **50-51**, **91**, **92**, **114**, 125
Rolfe, Frederick 17
Royals (company of the stockings) 124
Ruskin, John 10
Ruzante 20

Sacerdoti 17, **34**, **46-47**, 104
Salmistrari 22
San Francesco della Vigna **78-79**, **118**, 119
Sansovino, Francesco 55, 57, 72, 73, 80, 92, 125
Sanudo, Marin 85, 96
Savorgnan 73
Scalera film **148**
Scuola Grande di San Rocco 136, 138
Selvatico, Pietro 15, 25
Sen-Nefer 56
Simon, Santo 70
Sorian 73
Stucky, mulino **129**
Symonds, J.A. 22

Tagliapietra 31, **119**, 146
Tannhäuser 152
Tassini, Giuseppe 22, 26, 57, 98, 114, 131, 134, 136
Temanza, Tomaso 64, 149
Terra **30**, **84**, 119
Theophrastes 85
Tiepolo, former palazzo 22
Tintoretto, Jacopo 88
Titian 20, 56, 57, 73, 80, 138
Torres **88**
Trissino, Gian Luca 20
Tura, Cosmé 88
Twain, Mark 113

Ughi, Lodovico 17, 22, 31, 80

Vasari, Giorgio 125
Vaudoyer, Jean Louis 17, 138
Vendramin Calergi *see* Grimani
Vendramini 55
Venier (garden) 91
Venier, Maffeo 20
Veronese, Paolo 72
Vittoria, Alessandro 24, 72

Zaghis, Pietro 73
Zalterio, Bolognino 17, 20
Zane 64
Zieseniss **26**, 32, 56

The Sites

Abbazia della Misericordia 19
Altieri 2
Alverà 87
American hotel 66
Armenian College (Ca' Zenobio) 38
Artigianelli 62
Associazione Bocciofili 32
Balbi Valier 80
Balboni 50
Baldissera 97
Barbaro 81
Barbini 73
Barnabò 84
Barozzi 74
Barusco 79
Basadonna Recanati 59
Bastianello 30
Battistello 34
Bellinato 21
Bennati 86
Borsato 68
Brandolini d'Adda 57
Ca' Corner 89
Ca' Dario 77
Ca' Leon 110
Ca' Tron 11
Calzavara 72
Candiani 14
Cappello 25
Cardazzo 36
Carmelitani Scalzi 5
Casa Cardinal Piazza 17
Casa Frollo 112
Casa Madame Stern 58
Casellati 27
Casellati 69
Cassetti 44
Cavenago 35
Chiari 51
Cipriani 117
Clarisse 107
Contarini dal Zaffo (Casin dei Spiriti) 18
Contarini Porta di Ferro 94
Cosulich 41
Zieseniss 37
Croze 65
D'Annunzio 88
De Michelis 31
De Pol 106
Di Thiene 100
Donati 55
Enel 1
former Eden 111
former Palazzo Contarini 10
former Palazzo Tiepolo 20
Ferruzzi 52
Finanza 118
Fiorazzo 71
Fitzgerald 105

166

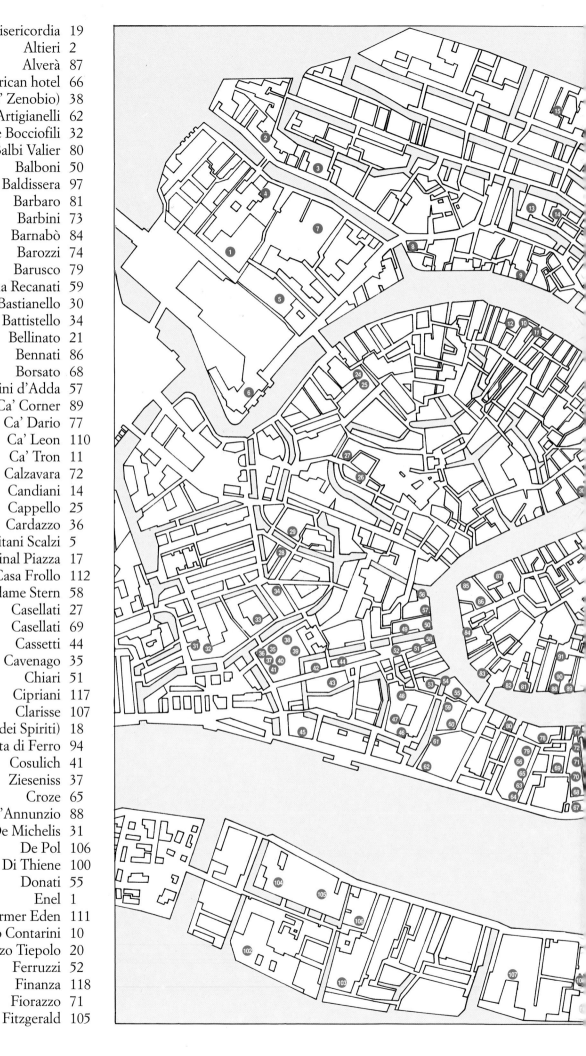

91	Foscari
82	Franchetti
45	Fullin
49	Gaggia
47	Giove
7	Gobbetto
104	Gozzi
24	Gradenigo
9	Grimani (Vendramin-Calergi)
78	Guggenheim
103	Herion
46	Höhs
115	Ire former Zitelle
43	Lazzarini
22	Levi-Morenos
6	Lion-Cavazza
42	Lorenzon
56	Lucheschi
70	Mainardis
83	Marcello
85	Mocenigo
40	Mocenigo Casagrande
48	Montin
114	Morelli
23	Morosini del Giardin
61	Nani Mocenigo
95	Ordine di Malta
3	Orsoni
12	Palazzo Belloni Battagia
54	Palazzo Contarini degli Scrigni
29	Palazzo Minotto
116	Palazzo Mocenigo Marcello
15	Patarol (former Della Vecchia)
96	Pellegrini
53	Pensione Accademia
4	Pinzocchere
90	Piva
99	Questura
108	Redentore
63	Rocca
64	Rusconi
109	Sacerdoti
26	Salmistrari
93	San Francesco della Vigna
102	Scalera Film
33	Scuola di Servizio Sociale
76	Seminario
13	Serviti
75	Simon Santo
39	Soccorso
8	Tagliapietra (former Querini Papozze)
60	Terra
28	Torres
67	Torzo
113	Tre Oci
101	Uberti
98	Ustino
92	Van Axel
16	Zennaro

167